NCAC® I and II Practice Questions

Mometrix

TEST PREPARATION

DEAR FUTURE EXAM SUCCESS STORY

First of all, **THANK YOU** for purchasing Mometrix study materials!

Second, congratulations! You are one of the few determined test-takers who are committed to doing whatever it takes to excel on your exam. **You have come to the right place.** We developed these practice tests with one goal in mind: to deliver you the best possible approximation of the questions you will see on test day.

Standardized testing is one of the biggest obstacles on your road to success, which only increases the importance of doing well in the high-pressure, high-stakes environment of test day. Your results on this test could have a significant impact on your future, and these practice tests will give you the repetitions you need to build your familiarity and confidence with the test content and format to help you achieve your full potential on test day.

Your success is our success

We would love to hear from you! If you would like to share the story of your exam success or if you have any questions or comments in regard to our products, please contact us at **800-673-8175** or **support@mometrix.com**.

Thanks again for your business and we wish you continued success!

Sincerely,
The Mometrix Test Preparation Team

Written and edited by the Mometrix Exam Secrets Test Prep Team
Printed in the United States of America

Table of Contents

Practice Test #1

1. Cannabis use disorder is associated with developing higher instances and/or worsening symptoms of which one of the following?

a. PTSD.
b. Obsessive-compulsive disorder.
c. Schizophrenia.
d. Attention-deficit hyperactivity disorder.

2. Examples of psychoactive drugs include all of the following EXCEPT:

a. opium.
b. caffeine.
c. aspirin.
d. nicotine

3. The "Five As" of tobacco treatment, in proper order, are:

a. Assess, advise, approve, advocate, and arrange
b. Ask, assess, assist, arrange, and advise
c. Ask, advise, assess, assist, and arrange
d. Assess, agree, assist, advocate, and approve

Refer to the following for questions 4-7:

Leon is a 33-year-old information technology systems administrator referred by his employer after a random drug screen and confirmatory drug test indicated the presence of THC. He was referred to his employee assistance program after a substance use screener yielded concerning results. The AP is meeting with Leon today to determine whether additional diagnostic assessments or evaluations are warranted.

The counselor learns that Leon identifies as a recovering alcoholic and says that he uses marijuana recreationally. He reports that there was a time in his life when he realized that combining marijuana and alcohol was causing problems, so he decided to quit drinking. Leon does not think he has a problem with cannabis use but consents to a diagnostic interview as part of his employee assistance program requirements.

During the interview, the therapist selects an instrument with cutoff scores, allowing for increased specificity and sensitivity. Leon is instructed to complete this eight-question self-administered questionnaire measuring his frequency of use within the past 6 months. This includes but is not limited to the time spent "stoned" in a typical day, the amount of time spent recovering, the ability to meet daily expectations, and engagement in physically hazardous activities while using. Leon was asked to provide a score from 1 to 5 representing the frequency of each inquiry. The therapist also performed a biopsychosocial assessment that yielded a provisional diagnosis of cannabis use disorder (CUD), moderate.

4. The primary function of Leon's screening for cannabis use is to determine whether:

a. he is at risk for or currently has use-related problems.
b. his severity of use warrants immediate attention.
c. his level of risk requires an alternate treatment setting.
d. he has protective factors that could mitigate his overall risk.

5. Which one of the following screening instruments did the counselor use?

a. DAST.
b. PCL-5.
c. CUDIT-2.
d. SDS.

6. The combination of cannabis and alcohol produces a(n):

a. antagonistic effect.
b. potentiation effect.
c. additive effect.
d. synergetic effect.

7. The DSM-5-TR specifies whether cannabis use disorder (CUD) is mild, moderate, or severe based on which one of the following?

a. The degree of functional impairment.
b. The presence of impaired control and risky use.
c. The results of testing instruments with reliable and valid subscales.
d. The total number of identified symptoms across multiple domains.

8. Doctor shopping is most closely associated with which one of the following?

a. Substance use.
b. Substance misuse.
c. Substance dependency.
d. Substance addiction.

9. Which one of the following is a screening tool designed for pregnant people?

a. The 5 Ps.
b. Substance Use Brief Screen.
c. The CRAFFT (which stands for car, relax, alone, forget, family or friends, trouble) instrument.
d. Tobacco, Alcohol, Prescription Medication, and Other Substance Use tool (TAPS).

10. Psychoactive drugs are drugs that:

a. alter behavior or mood.
b. alter only mood.
c. alter only behavior.
d. have little or no effect on mood or behavior.

11. Several mandatory disclosures must be provided during informed consent, including all of the following EXCEPT:

a. APs must inform clients of their right to refuse services.
b. APs must provide a general overview of treatment services.
c. APs must review confidentiality and its limits, including duty to warn.
d. APs must inform clients of their billing procedures, including fees and nonpayment policies.

12. An employee receives a positive result on a urine drug screen. The employer can infer which one of the following from this test?

a. The amount of substance used.
b. The substances used in the employee's lifetime.
c. The detection of drug metabolites.
d. Confirmation of any substances used or misused.

13. The Addiction Severity Index has been formally adopted by which organization?

a. The Substance Abuse and Mental Health Services Administration (SAMHSA)
b. The Center on Drug and Alcohol Research (CDAR)
c. The National Institute on Drug Abuse (NIDA)
d. The Institute for Governmental Service and Research (IGSR)

14. A great deal is communicated nonverbally in the counseling process. How much communication does nonverbal body language account for, according to research?

a. 10 percent
b. 25 percent
c. 50 percent
d. 75 percent

15. APs who find themselves in unavoidable dual relationships take precautions to prevent client harm, including all of the following EXCEPT:

a. obtaining informed consent.
b. complying with duty to warn.
c. documenting treatment recommendations.
d. seeking consultation or supervision.

16. According to Principle II-1 of the NAADAC Code of Ethics (2021), clients participating in which one of the following have the right to know what information is exchanged and with whom?

a. Multidimensional assessments.
b. Multicultural treatment.
c. Multidisciplinary care.
d. Multipronged interventions.

17. Boundary violations consist of dual relationships that are:

a. unavoidable.
b. exploitative.
c. unintentional.
d. irreconcilable.

18. Sooner or later, all treatment programs end, and a discharge summary and continuing care plan will then be required. What is the key difference between a discharge summary and a continuing care plan?

a. A discharge plan provides directions for further treatment, while the continuing care plan addresses the client's clinical presentation at discharge.
b. A discharge plan provides an overview of treatment and outcomes, while the continuing care plan addresses aftercare options based on the client's response to treatment.
c. A discharge plan provides a roster of prior professionals involved, while the continuing care plan proposes further professionals to engage in the treatment process.
d. A discharge plan provides a theoretical orientation to a client's presentation, while a continuing care plan offers a model for further intervention.

19. Culture can play a significant role in substance abuse. How do Hispanic and Latino populations, in general, tend to respond to alcohol problems in the family?

a. By lashing out and aggressively confronting the drinking problem
b. By attempting to ignore and avoid discussing the drinking problem
c. By seeking out authority figures to help them engage the drinking problem
d. By seeking out religious leaders to help them engage the drinking problem

20. Which of the following instruments is used to screen for substance use in individuals who are either unwilling or unable to concede to problematic use.

a. MAST
b. SASSI
c. SBIRT
d. ASI

Refer to the following for questions 21-24:

Tyler is an 11-year-old male referred for outpatient therapy after he and a group of others were suspended for substance use. Tyler is accompanied by his father, who stays at home with Tyler's three younger siblings during the day. The school counselor has faxed a signed release, enabling the therapist to gather information before the initial interview.

The therapist learns that Tyler is frequently in the nurse's office complaining of stomachaches and headaches. He tends to walk the halls with his head down and is quick to cry and prone to angry outbursts. School personnel are aware of instances of bullying, particularly on Tyler's bus, but they maintain that they are difficult to pinpoint or monitor. Tyler has tried repeatedly to gain the acceptance of his peers, some of whom are older and regarded as negative influences. Recently, Tyler's bus driver caught Tyler and his peers using whipped cream propellant canisters (whippets) to get high.

During Tyler's session with his outpatient therapist, he states that his peers dared him to do whippets and other substances, stating, "They would hold me down if I wouldn't. These same guys also made me take a pill that they said was Molly." His father reports ongoing bullying, and he is considering placing Tyler in an alternative school. Although he believes Tyler is being bullied, he does not believe he was forced to engage in drug use, stating, "He'll do just about anything for attention and approval."

21. Research on the reasons why youths initiate substance use include all of the following EXCEPT:

a. the belief that they will gain peer support.
b. the belief that they will have a pleasurable experience.
c. the belief that they will not have adverse consequences.
d. the belief that they will improve work, school, or sports performance.

22. In addition to inhalants, Tyler also reports taking:

a. PCP.
b. MDMA.
c. LSD.
d. GHB.

23. To meet the standards of the definition of bullying the action CANNOT be:

a. indirect.
b. contextual.
c. relational.
d. unintentional.

24. Inhalants obtained from whipped cream propellant canisters (whippets) are categorized as:

a. gases.
b. nitrites.
c. aerosols.
d. volatile solvents.

25. In the DSM-5-TR, the severity of substance use disorder (SUD) is determined by the:

a. number of symptoms present.
b. degree of functional impairment.
c. existence of withdrawal or dependence.
d. number of substance-related consequences.

26. Sudden sniffing death is a fatal condition associated with inhalant use and is caused by which of the following?

a. Lung failure.
b. Pancreas failure.
c. Kidney failure.
d. Heart failure.

27. A client diagnosed with alcohol use disorder and major depressive disorder has been sober for seven months but continues to require counseling for relapse prevention and problem-solving. Although successful with sobriety, the client continues to present with feelings of worthlessness and anhedonia. This best relates to which of the following stages of readiness to change?

a. Contemplation
b. Maintenance
c. Preparation
d. Termination.

28. About half of individuals who experience a seizure during alcohol withdrawal will develop which one of the following?

a. Hyperreflexia.
b. Delirium tremens.
c. Anhedonia.
d. Insomnia.

29. Traditionally, what has the term *therapeutic community (TC)* referred to?

a. An informal group organized for mutual support
b. A court-ordered treatment environment
c. A formal mutual-help or twelve-step support group
d. A drug-free residential treatment environment

30. Which one of the following is a four-item screening tool for unhealthy use of tobacco, alcohol, illicit substances, and prescription drugs among adults?

a. Addiction Severity Index.
b. Substance Use Brief Screen.
c. Drug Abuse Screening Test.
d. Screening to Brief Intervention.

31. Factors contributing to behavioral health disparities among diverse populations include which one of the following?

a. Individual health choices.
b. Social determinants of health.
c. An inability to persevere amid hardship.
d. Misuse of equally distributed resources.

32. The NAADAC Ethics Committee can only accept complaints and grievances that fall within their scope of oversight, including which one of the following?

a. Anonymous complaints.
b. Wrongful business practice claims.
c. Civil complaints involving financial restitution.
d. Failure to use evidence-based practices.

Refer to the following for questions 33-36:

Gang, who prefers to be called John, is a 43-year-old male receiving inpatient treatment for AUD and major depressive disorder. John's evaluation shows that he was initially classified as being in quadrant IV of the Four Quadrants Model of care. He has been at the treatment center for 60 days and has begun to show improvements. John has been assigned a new counselor, who is familiarizing themselves with his medical record.

The counselor learns that John was recently divorced after 20 years of marriage. His records indicate that this was the result of his wife's infidelity. He is a second-generation Chinese American, and the divorce became a source of shame for him. During that time, John became depressed, and his alcohol consumption increased. He later tells the counselor, "My birth name is 'Gang,' which is my grandfather's name. It means 'strong warrior,' and here I was, unable to get out of bed unless it was to get blackout drunk. I began to hate the person I had become. It got to the point that I didn't care whether I lived or died."

John's medical record shows that he required medical detoxification upon admission. He experienced withdrawal seizures but did not go on to experience delirium tremens. John agreed to be placed on an FDA-approved medication for AUD and has begun to understand that he cannot overcome his addiction with willpower. He knows that if he drinks while on the medication, he will experience unpleasant side effects, including vomiting, chest pain, and difficulty breathing. He has begun earning privileges, attending outside meetings, and receiving visitors. John was attracted to the treatment center because it offered yoga and meditation, a culturally traditional practice that John once valued but had relinquished once his drinking and depression worsened.

33. The Four Quadrants Model of care is a classification system involving all of the following EXCEPT:

a. level of care.
b. clinical diagnosis.
c. treatment setting.
d. symptom severity.

34. What percentage of individuals experiencing seizures from alcohol withdrawal go on to experience delirium tremens?

a. 25%.
b. 50%.
c. 75%.
d. 100%.

35. John's use of yoga and meditation is classified as which form of treatment?

a. Alternative.
b. Behavioral.
c. Conventional.
d. Complementary.

36. Which FDA-approved medication has John been prescribed for AUD, based on the description of its side effects when taken with alcohol?

a. Naltrexone.
b. Acamprosate.
c. Disulfiram.
d. Methadone.

37. Which of the following is FDA-approved to treat opioid use disorder?

a. buprenorphine
b. topiramate
c. acamprosate
d. disulfiram

38. How is the concept of culture BEST described?

a. A shared set of beliefs, norms, and values among a racial group
b. A shared set of beliefs, norms, and values among an ethnic group
c. A shared set of beliefs, norms, and values among any given group
d. A shared set of beliefs, norms, and values among a given nationality

Refer to the following for questions 39-42:

Fran is a 48-year-old female entering treatment for prescription opioid misuse. This is her third inpatient admission. Her husband accompanies her today and relays that he has become increasingly concerned over Fran mixing prescription opioids and alcohol. He reports arriving home "most nights to find Fran slurring her words or passed out in front of the television." Fran states that she has a prescription for opioids, which she takes for chronic pain and insomnia. She explains that they are moderately effective and that combining them with alcohol helps her to relax and fall asleep.

The counselor determines that Fran has a long history of depression and PTSD. Fran reports that her mother died when she was 4, leaving her to live with her father until she ran away with her boyfriend at age 17. She states, "I never finished high school. I became pregnant and was excited about having my own family. My boyfriend was abusive, and as a result, I lost the baby." She has been married to her second husband for 5 years, and they are "surrogate parents" for their grandchildren. She states, "I finally get to parent for the first time at my age"—a role she has found fulfilling.

The counselor provides an in-depth assessment and evaluation. Fran completes the Adverse Childhood Experiences (ACEs) Questionnaire, and the counselor uses the results to help Fran develop insight into the impact of trauma on her substance misuse. Although Fran is open to processing her ACEs, she remains resistant to change her substance use. The counselor will take a harm reduction approach and use motivational enhancement therapy and trauma-informed care.

39. Which one of the following is NOT true of adverse childhood experiences (ACEs)?

a. They include child abuse and neglect.
b. They include witnessing violence.
c. They impact a child's safety and security.
d. They occur before a child's 16th birthday.

40. Research indicates that ACEs Questionnaire scores are highest among individuals who are all of the following EXCEPT:

a. male.
b. non-Hispanic white.
c. unemployed.
d. children with older parents.

41. Fran's ACEs Questionnaire scores illustrate that, when left untreated, the excessive, prolonged, and chronic effects of ACEs can have lifelong consequences. This is due to the relationship between ACEs and:

a. toxic stress.
b. positive stress.
c. neurological stress.
d. tolerable stress.

42. The counselor helps Fran develop discrepancy as part of motivational enhancement therapy by examining the differences between her:

a. sustain talk and change talk.
b. resistance and cooperation.
c. values and behaviors.
d. put-downs and affirmations.

43. Life-threatening withdrawal symptoms can occur with all of the following substances EXCEPT:

a. alcohol.
b. cocaine.
c. opioids.
d. sedatives.

Refer to the following for questions 44-47:

Jack is a 4-year-old male referred by his pediatrician for early childhood services. He is accompanied by his 22-year-old mother, Zoe, who is a single parent. Zoe explains that she is newly sober and wishes to break the cycle of intergenerational substance abuse. The counselor constructs a genogram with Zoe and discovers several family members with problematic drug and alcohol use, including both parents, a maternal grandparent, and one of Zoe's siblings. Zoe describes growing up in an unstable home environment with few socioeconomic resources. Child protective services briefly removed Zoe from her home for physical abuse when she was in kindergarten.

The counselor reviews Jack's developmental milestones. She learns that Jack has difficulty self-soothing when frustrated and that he has language and cognitive delays. Jack's bedtime is particularly difficult, with Zoe admitting that she allows Jack to sleep in bed with her if he "starts to throw a tantrum." Zoe describes her parenting style as strict, but she has had difficulty keeping Jack on a set schedule. She states that she disciplines Jack by using spankings and time-outs.

Zoe is in contact with her parents but says they are "uninterested in having a relationship with Jack." Zoe believes it is because she and Jack have similar temperaments, explaining, "My mom says I was also a handful at that age." Zoe states that parenting while sober has been challenging, but she loves her son and desires a better life for him. The counselor plans to adhere to evidence-based prevention and intervention principles by targeting proximal factors, identifying protective influences, and improving parent–child interactions.

44. Which one of the following parenting styles is least likely to serve as a risk factor for developing SUD?

a. Uninvolved.
b. Authoritarian.
c. Authoritative.
d. Permissive.

45. Which one of the following is a family risk factor for developing AUD?

a. Family cohesion.
b. Both parents having full-time employment.
c. Adequate socioeconomic resources.
d. Secure attachment.

46. Which one of the following serves as a protective factor for this family?

a. Zoe's parenting style.
b. Zoe's help-seeking behavior.
c. Jack's temperament.
d. Jack's school readiness.

47. Which one of the following is a proximal risk factor for developing SUD?

a. Genetics.
b. Temperament.
c. Family history.
d. Family environment.

48. Risk factors for contracting hepatitis C virus include all of the following EXCEPT:

a. HIV.
b. hepatitis B virus.
c. kidney disease.
d. fatty liver disease.

49. You find that recording therapy sessions works well for you. Which is true of an AP's ethical responsibility for recording therapy?

a. The AP must obtain informed consent and releases of information prior to recording.
b. The AP must obtain informed consent only prior to recording.
c. The AP must obtain releases of information only prior to recording.
d. The AP need not obtain informed consent nor releases of information prior to recording.

Refer to the following for questions 50-54:

Zia is a 25-year-old female who meets with her AP today for the first time via a secure e-therapy video platform. Zia has been diagnosed with panic disorder and reports that she made progress with her previous therapist, but she had to stop going after starting a new full-time job. Zia says that she is drawn to e-therapy after a recent increase in anxiety made it difficult for her to leave the house. She expresses feeling anxious in enclosed spaces and crowds and tries to avoid going to new places. Zia also indicates that, whenever possible, she will have a few drinks before leaving the house "just to take the edge off."

The AP begins the session by executing informed consent and ensuring that Zia understands the risks and benefits of e-therapy. Zia says she was surprised that her initial appointment was scheduled within 48 hours, explaining, "I called and hung up several times before making the appointment. It is embarrassing to share that I'm having difficulty leaving my house." The AP responds, "It took a lot of courage for you to follow through with the appointment. That's a big first step!"

The AP explains that she is newly hired and under close supervision, which requires direct observation and consultation with a treatment team. Because the counseling sessions are online, the AP has been asked to provide video recordings for each e-therapy session. Zia was provided with the name of the AP's supervisor and told that she could withdraw permission at any time. She agrees to the AP videotaping the session and verbalizes that she is motivated to learn new ways to reduce her anxiety and alcohol consumption. The AP obtains detailed information on how she made progress with her last therapist to incorporate Zia's strengths into her current treatment plan.

50. Zia was able to quickly schedule an initial intake appointment. This is associated with reduced client:

a. access.
b. outcomes.
c. dropout rates.
d. autonomy.

51. An informed consent for e-therapy should include all of the following EXCEPT:

a. social media policies.
b. emergency protocols.
c. synchronous communication response time.
d. procedures for when the counselor is unavailable.

52. In-person counseling is superior to e-therapy in terms of upholding and maintaining:

a. privilege.
b. confidentiality.
c. standards of practice.
d. professional responsibilities.

53. The AP's response to Zia's hesitancy and embarrassment associated with scheduling her initial appointment is an example of a(n):

a. affirmation.
b. reflection.
c. clarification.
d. empathetic statement.

54. According to the NAADAC Code of Ethics (2021), before videotaping an e-therapy session, the AP must obtain:

a. specialized training and preapproved methods for video storage.
b. a virtual private network and an approved client safety plan.
c. informed consent and releases of information permitting third-party observation.
d. client consent and Health Insurance Portability and Accountability Act of 1996 (HIPAA) and 42 Code of Federal Regulations Part 2 approval.

55. The sedative effects of alcohol are caused by activation of the primary inhibitory neurotransmitter known as:

a. epinephrine.
b. acetylcholine.
c. gamma-aminobutyric acid (GABA).
d. norepinephrine.

56. Which one of the following refers to the process in which a client's eligibility for a treatment program or intervention is identified?

a. Evaluation
b. Assessment.
c. Referral.
d. Screening.

57. According to Principle I-40 of the NAADAC Code of Ethics (2021), before accepting or declining gifts from clients, APs must:

a. evaluate the client's ability to afford the gift.
b. consider the cultural implications.
c. inform clients of the ethical implications at the outset of treatment.
d. obtain supervision or consultation and document recommendations.

Refer to the following for questions 58-61:

Max is an AP conducting a research study on AUD. Specifically, Max seeks to determine the effectiveness of behavioral health therapy and Alcoholics Anonymous (AA) on AUD outcomes.

There are two treatment groups in Max's experimental design: Group A receives behavioral health therapy, while group B receives behavioral health therapy and also must attend weekly AA meetings. Group B must provide proof of attendance by submitting a document with each participant's name and the AA chairperson's signature. Patient-reported outcome measures will be gathered to measure participants' abstinence status, functional status, and quality of life. The measures will be collected monthly for 3 months.

Max provides outpatient addiction treatment at an agency with other behavioral health providers. He determines that all new intakes who agree to participate in the study will be randomly assigned to either group A or group B. Group B is given gift cards as compensation for the additional requirement of attending AA meetings. Max explains that all data and identifying information will be kept confidential and that participants' privacy and anonymity will be protected.

During data collection, Max encounters numerous questions and concerns. Group B members question whether their participation in AA or the identity of the chairperson will remain anonymous because they are required to submit a signed attendance sheet. Group A discovers that group B is receiving incentives and complains that this is unfair. There are also some participants in group A who became interested in AA and question the value of waiting until the completion of the study (3 months) to begin.

Max responds to each concern. He agrees to provide incentives to both groups and arranges to remove any identifying information from the AA attendance sheet. Group A's concern over the inability to attend AA was addressed during the debriefing. At this time, Max reveals that group A was paired with more experienced therapists, thus ensuring that their treatment needs would not go unmet and any harm from not attending AA would be minimized. Max stated that he knowingly withheld this information for the good of the study.

The following week, Max discovers that a colleague has made an ethics complaint/grievance against him with the NAADAC.

58. In the context of research studies, confidentiality is best reviewed:

a. at predetermined intervals.
b. at the client's discretion.
c. when debriefing research participants.
d. at the beginning of the research study.

59. APs conducting anonymous research studies are ethically responsible for protecting the anonymity of participants. This is accomplished by:

a. protecting a subject's identifiable data.
b. collecting only essential information.
c. protecting unauthorized access to research data.
d. refraining from collecting personal identifiers.

60. Which is true of deceptive research practices, such as that done by Max?

a. Deception is never permissible and should be avoided at all times.
b. Deception is always permissible unless it involves coercion or exploitation.
c. Deception is only permissible if it is essential to the research protocol and approved by an institutional review board or human subjects committee.
d. Deception is only permissible if it is essential to the research protocol and approved by a supervisor or consultant.

61. If the ethical complaint with NAADAC is found to be valid against Max, all of the following may occur EXCEPT:

a. revocation of his NAADAC membership.
b. termination of his certification or licensure.
c. requests for him to attend an ethics training.
d. dismissal of the case if malpractice cannot be proven.

62. Which one of the following steps involves obtaining information on an ongoing basis to help formulate a clinical diagnosis and determine the direction of treatment?

a. Orientation.
b. Assessment.
c. Intake.
d. Screening.

63. Which of the following is an evidence-based practice based on the work of Prochaska and DiClemente's Stages of Change model?

a. Cognitive-behavioral therapy
b. Contingency management
c. Motivational interviewing
d. Person-centered therapy

64. What is the case management model that integrates therapeutic and resource acquisition activities known as?

a. Strengths-Based Perspective
b. Clinical or Rehabilitation Model
c. Brokerage or Generalist model
d. Program of Assertive Community Treatment Model

65. Which of the following functions is NOT what a Certified Alcohol and Drug Abuse Counselor can usually perform?

a. Client screening
b. Substance use assessment
c. Diagnose mental disorders
d. Formulate a treatment plan

66. For counselors working with clients in crisis, differentiating between substance-induced mood disorders and independent (i.e., singular) mood disorders is critical because:

a. suicide rates are highest among those with independent mood disorders.
b. pharmacological treatment is not recommended for substance-induced mood disorders.
c. medically monitored withdrawal must be used with substance-induced mood disorders.
d. collateral support is essential when treating a substance-induced mood disorder.

67. The therapeutic relationship can produce feelings that are challenging. What does the term *countertransference* refer to?

a. Feelings from the client that are projected onto the counselor
b. Feelings from the counselor that are projected onto the client
c. Feelings that the client openly shares with the counselor
d. Feelings from the counselor that are used to promote resolution

68. How is the proper role for mental health medications in individuals with co-occurring disorders BEST described?

a. There is no place for mental health medications in the treatment of clients with a substance abuse problem.
b. Clients with a substance abuse disorder and a co-occurring mental health disorder can benefit from medications.
c. Clients with a substance abuse disorder and a co-occurring mental health disorder can take mental health medications without any concern.
d. Clients with a substance abuse disorder and a co-occurring mental health disorder will always benefit from long-term pharmacotherapy.

69. Parents engaging in substance use are often unresponsive to their child's needs. Which of the following BEST provides a theoretical framework for understanding associated consequences?

a. Change theory
b. Behavioral theory
c. Attachment theory
d. Circular communications theory

70. Using the ASAM multidimensional assessment, which dimension incorporates the transtheoretical model of behavioral change?

a. Readiness to change.
b. Recovering/Living environment.
c. Emotional, behavioral, and cognitive conditions and complications.
d. Relapse, continued use, or continued problem potential.

71. Tracking client progress longitudinally is important to measure progress and document program effectiveness. How often is client data typically reviewed?

a. Annually
b. Biannually
c. Semiannually
d. Quarterly

72. When compared to their male counterparts, females ages 12–21 who drink alcohol have higher instances of all the following EXCEPT:

a. alcohol-related deaths.
b. alcohol-related blackouts.
c. alcohol-related liver cancer.
d. alcohol-related heart disease.

73. Which of the following is the BEST description of a drug?

a. A substance (other than food) taken for a desired biological effect.
b. A substance used to mitigate, prevent, or treat a disease.
c. A substance used to produce a high.
d. A substance that can have both positive and negative effects.

74. There are numerous methods used to encourage a substance abuser to enter treatment. Who carries out a programmed confrontation?

a. A trained addictions counselor
b. A primary care physician
c. A psychotherapist
d. A family member

75. Clinicians use the "ask-tell-ask" technique to optimize client responsiveness and investment in treatment. Which of the following best demonstrates this technique?

a. "Do you have any questions?"
b. "Do you understand the information?"
c. "Can you explain what we have discussed?"
d. "Can you let someone know if you have questions?

76. Which one of the following populations has the highest rate of SUDs?

a. White people.
b. Hispanic or Latino people.
c. Native American or Alaskan Native people.
d. Black or African American people.

77. How is the term *genogram* BEST defined?

a. A diagram of family relationships
b. A genetic predisposition to addiction
c. A pictogram of intergenerational addiction
d. A phenotype predisposing alcoholism

78. Formerly known as the COPES, The Community Oriented Program Environment Scale (CPES) measures which of the following?

a. Continuity of care in residential settings.
b. Client support and community resources.
c. Transtheoretical stages of change.
d. Social climate and program perceptions.

79. APs demonstrate their scope of practice through all of the following EXCEPT:

a. specialized education and training in addiction counseling.
b. supervised experience in addiction counseling.
c. evidence-based practices for addiction disorders.
d. skills required to deliver addiction-specific services.

80. The term *authentically connected referral network* is BEST described as which of the following?

a. An online resource portal for available community services.
b. A set of defined relationships able to adapt and flexibly meet client needs
c. A referral system created to address post-treatment aftercare and follow up.
d. An informal consortium of providers sharing information with one another.

81. This group model is grounded in the assumption that substance use originates from actions that are learned and reinforced over time?

a. Psychoeducational group type
b. Behavioral group type
c. Interpersonal process group type
d. Support group type

82. Client assessment, evaluation, and need for referrals should be ongoing as discovered. When should planning for aftercare be engaged?

a. During the last few sessions, addressing specific needs
b. When a client is roughly halfway through a program
c. After measurable progress has been demonstrated
d. At the point of the initial counselor-client contact

83. Adjunctive therapies refer to all EXCEPT which of the following?

a. Vocational training
b. Stress management
c. Meditation
d. Acupuncture

Refer to the following for questions 84-87:

Amy is a 32-year-old female referred to an AP to be evaluated for amphetamine and stimulant use. Amy has received ongoing therapy for PTSD, and her provider recommended the evaluation. Amy is greeted by her provider, Karen, a 45-year-old female who resides in the surrounding metropolitan area. Karen understands that Amy has experienced physical abuse and intimate partner violence. The referral indicates that Amy is a single parent who resides with her two children just outside of her American Indian tribal community. Karen, a non-Native provider, has worked closely with members of Amy's tribe and understands that trust must be gained and that early engagement is critical for improved outcomes.

Amy's substance abuse evaluation indicates that she uses amphetamines nearly every day. She reports that she drinks alcohol periodically and smokes two packs of cigarettes a day. Each morning, Amy has 3–4 cups of coffee. Karen notes that Amy has tried to quit smoking but has never been successful. She states, "I smoked through both of my pregnancies, and I have an immense degree of shame over it." Karen seeks to understand the source of her shame and how it also connects to her previous experiences of trauma and abuse.

Karen explores Amy's cultural identity and the significance of her traditional Native activities, values, and beliefs. Karen is aware of her own biases and attitudes and is grounded in cultural humility. Discussions around cross-cultural experiences are intentionally introduced, and there is an open dialogue on the similarities and differences (including power differentials) between both cultures. In her work with Karen, Amy was able to reconnect with her traditional teachings and identify steps that would enable her to begin to walk in peace, balance, and harmony. She responded well to a harm reduction model, a mindfulness-based approach for stimulant misuse. Karen's ability to actively listen and acknowledge power differentials resulted in a strong therapeutic alliance and improved outcomes for Amy.

84. Which one of the following is classified as a synthetic substance?

a. Caffeine.
b. Nicotine.
c. Cocaine.
d. Amphetamine.

85. The cultural identities of American Indians/Alaska Natives are characterized by all of the following EXCEPT:

a. they remain static across time.
b. they are historically formed.
c. they are grounded in respect for their elders.
d. they are influenced by generational stories.

86. Attributes of cultural humility include all of the following EXCEPT:

a. openness.
b. expertise.
c. authenticity.
d. self-awareness.

87. Karen practices cultural humility by intentionally discussing cross-cultural experiences and the similarities and differences in their cultures through a process known as:

a. breaking.
b. bridging.
c. broaching.
d. brokering.

88. How is motivational enhancement therapy (MET) different from motivational interviewing (MI)?

a. MET incorporates structured assessments and follow-up sessions.
b. MET is more unstructured and free-flowing as compared with MI.
c. MET is entirely reflective and non-determinative as compared with MI.
d. MET requires considerable confrontation and counselor assertiveness.

89. Which one of the following describes the unjust use of social power to deprive subgroups of the resources needed to lead safe, healthy, and productive lives?

a. Prejudice.
b. Racism.
c. Oppression.
d. Microaggressions.

Refer to the following for questions 90-93:

Caleb is a 19-year-old male who presents to the emergency department (ED) after his roommate called 911. Caleb is agitated and verbally combative upon arrival. He is observed pacing the hallways, breathing heavily, and yelling, "I can't stay here because I'm being followed!" At other times, Caleb rambles, displays disorganized thinking, and appears to be responding to auditory hallucinations. A friend who accompanies Caleb explains that Caleb started using methamphetamine (MA) heavily approximately 9 months ago and binges for several days at a time "whenever he can get his hands on it."

The intake clinician provides an assessment once the intoxication subsides. Caleb is reluctant to engage with the counselor, stating, "My last counselor was also an older white woman. I think she had it out for young black men." However, with some encouragement, Caleb participates in the interview. He reports using alcohol, stimulants, and nicotine. He explains that he used substances recreationally until he found MA. His use became more frequent at this time, and he began smoking it to enhance euphoria. He explains that his roommate is not his partner, that he is heterosexual, but he has sex with his roommate to obtain MA. Caleb reports that they have unprotected "chemsex" and have exchanged sex with other men for drugs.

Caleb reports that his father is serving a 10-year prison term for possession of marijuana and trafficking and manufacturing MA. Caleb's mother has been diagnosed with bipolar disorder. He explains that he is a momma's boy and will do almost anything to avoid disappointing her. Caleb is an only child. He relays that he has had to be the man of the house because his father is in and out of prison.

Caleb states that his feelings can be "like a roller coaster—up one day and down the next." When he is down, he endorses anhedonia, hypersomnolence, irritability, and depressed mood. Six months ago, Caleb began to see a counselor for depression, psychosis, and mood lability. His records show that he was diagnosed with bipolar disorder and schizophrenia and that he refused to take antipsychotic medication to treat those conditions. As a result, he was discharged for treatment noncompliance. The counselor uses American Society of Addiction Medicine (ASAM) principles and criteria, including harm reduction, to direct Caleb's treatment.

90. In the scenario, structural racism is most evident in all areas EXCEPT:

a. Caleb's psychiatric diagnoses.
b. Caleb's father's prison sentence.
c. Caleb's discharge summary.
d. Caleb's relationship with his mother.

91. The American Society of Addiction Medicine (ASAM) principles and criteria are designed to match all of the following EXCEPT:

a. the client's level of safety with the appropriate intensity of services.
b. the client's complex needs with integrated care.
c. the client's clinical diagnosis with the least restrictive setting.
d. the client's autonomy with ongoing service planning.

92. Which one of the following harm reduction strategies would be most beneficial to Caleb?

a. A needle exchange program.
b. Methadone treatment
c. Postexposure prophylaxis.
d. A mutually agreed-upon safety plan.

93. Evidence-based practices for the treatment of stimulant use disorder include all of the following EXCEPT:

a. contingency management.
b. US Food and Drug Administration (FDA)-approved medications.
c. cognitive-behavioral therapy.
d. motivational interviewing.

94. Which one of the following is an advantage of using the Child and Adolescent Level of Care/Service Intensity Utilization System (CALOCUS-CASII)?

a. It can help with early recognition of treatment issues.
b. It can prescribe a specific treatment plan or environment.
c. It can be used in place of a comprehensive clinical assessment.
d. It can provide a clinical diagnosis for substance use and co-occurring disorders.

95. What have efficacy studies of the Matrix Model of treatment found?

a. The model is no more effective than other treatment programs.
b. The model is neutral in outcome efficacy.
c. The model is marginally positive in terms of efficacy.
d. The model is significantly positive in measures of efficacy.

96. Guidelines for managing access to a client's electronic health record include all of the following EXCEPT:

a. two-factor authentication.
b. a secure password.
c. effective media sanitation processes.
d. limited access (i.e., a need-to-know basis).

97. Which of the following does NOT require a written authorization to disclose confidential information?

a. A client's confirmed enrollment in a treatment program.
b. A client's confirmed substance use disorder diagnosis.
c. A report of suspected child abuse or neglect.
d. A report to an employer paying for treatment.

98. What of the following is NOT a key component in a treatment plan?

a. Problem statements from the intake assessment
b. Goal statements derived from problem statements
c. Objectives, which are what the client will do to meet treatment goals
d. Homework assignments to improve goal attainment

99. Which of the following is an example of a psychoactive substance's psychological effect?

a. Lethargy.
b. Delusions.
c. Itching.
d. Dizziness.

100. How does motivation for participating in treatment differ from motivation to change problem behaviors?

a. There is no difference between treatment and behavior change motivation.
b. Motivation for behavioral change precedes motivation for treatment.
c. Motivation for change is internal; treatment may be pushed on a client.
d. Motivation for treatment precedes motivation for behavioral change.

101. The DSM-5-TR recognizes substance-related and addictive disorders that change the brain's structure and reinforce repeated use. Of the substances recognized in the DSM-5-TR, the most common withdrawal symptom is:

a. fatigue.
b. psychomotor agitation.
c. vomiting.
d. emotional distress.

102. What is the factor that contributes MOST meaningfully to client treatment retention?

a. Program location and transportation support
b. The therapeutic alliance
c. Family insistence on treatment
d. Court orders for treatment

103. Addiction providers (AP) are responsible for making referrals for clients with impairments outside the AP's scope of practice. Specifically, APs are ethically responsible for ensuring that the resources are

a. financially appropriate.
b. Linguistically appropriate.
c. educationally appropriate.
d. administratively appropriate.

104. Which of the following is true of community reinforcement training (CRT) and contingency management (CM) approaches?

a. CRT and CM are most effective when paired together.
b. CRT and CM are not enduringly effective.
c. CRT is labor intensive, and CM can be costly.
d. CRT requires others' support, and CM requires ongoing rewards.

105. In planning a client's treatment based on assessment results, the client's problems, immediate and longer-term goals, measurable objectives, and treatment methods should be:

a. decided by the therapist with the client's agreement.
b. decided through a mutual client-therapist agreement.
c. decided by the client with the therapist's agreement.
d. decided for client and therapist by clinic's agreement.

106. A middle school student undergoes alcohol screening and brief intervention. During the screening, the student states that he does not drink alcohol but his friends drink. The counselor replies, "You are around friends who drink, yet you do not. Tell me a bit more about that." This is an example of:

a. probing.
b. summarizing.
c. clarification.
d. confirmation.

107. Which one of the following is an evidence-based treatment for pregnant people with OUD?

a. Buprenorphine and methadone treatment is recommended and is safe for the mother and fetus.
b. Medically supervised withdrawal from opioids is recommended and is safe for the mother and fetus.
c. Breastfeeding while taking buprenorphine or methadone is unsafe and is not advised.
d. Changing from buprenorphine to methadone during pregnancy is unsafe.

108. The study of pharmacokinetics includes all of the following processes EXCEPT:

a. absorption.
b. tolerance.
c. metabolism.
d. excretion.

109. A client receiving treatment for substance use disorder is issued a subpoena for confidential treatment records as part of a criminal investigation. According to the Code of Federal Regulations, Title 42, Part 2, Subpart E, the subpoena is:

a. Sufficient for release of information, provided it is delivered by a law officer
b. Sufficient for information release, if signed by a federal court judge
c. Insufficient for information release, unless signed by two qualified judges
d. Insufficient, unless a qualified hearing is first held in court

110. Bruce Tuckman proposed a model of group development that included five phases. What is the one phase that is NOT part of Tuckman's model?

a. Performing
b. Storming
c. Framing
d. Norming

111. Which one of the following questions can be found on the Addiction Severity Index?

a. "In the past two weeks, have you been bothered by poor appetite or overeating?"
b. "How often during the past year have you failed to do what was normally expected of you because of drinking?"
c. "Have you had blackouts or flashbacks as the result of drug use?"
d. "How many times in your life have you been charged with driving while intoxicated?"

Refer to the following for questions 112-115:

Tre is a 12-year-old 7th-grader referred by a juvenile court judge for status offenses that include alcohol use, possession of a controlled substance, and truancy. The judge refrained from formally filing charges and instead ordered Tre to comply with random drug screens and participate in family therapy. Although this is Tre's first criminal charge, he has an extensive mental health history, including treatment for reactive attachment disorder, PTSD, ADHD, and intellectual developmental disorder. Tre and his maternal grandmother present for an initial intake today. His grandmother provides signed consent to treatment; however, Tre refuses to provide signed assent agreeing to participate in therapy.

Tre's grandmother discloses that he was removed from his mother's care at age 3 after she was imprisoned for trafficking marijuana. Tre first saw a psychiatrist in the first grade and was prescribed an antipsychotic. He was unable to tolerate the side effects and was subsequently placed on an antidepressant and stimulant medication, which he no longer takes. Tre admits to frequent binge drinking and using marijuana, which appears to be primarily motivated by peer approval. The therapist works with Tre to identify cues or triggers associated with substance use.

The therapist provides psychoeducation to the grandmother, including the cycle of addiction and how addiction affects the brain's neurological pathways. Tre receives individual school-based therapy as part of a truancy diversion program. He continues to receive family therapy and awaits a follow-up psychiatric evaluation. The judge has requested that the therapist supply the court with a treatment summary; however, she is unable to submit the report because Tre's grandmother has yet to pay for prior services.

112. Before providing family therapy, the therapist must first determine if the:

a. client has the desire to change.
b. grandmother has legal guardianship.
c. client has the capacity to legally consent to treatment.
d. grandmother will be an active participant in therapy.

113. The addiction process involves all of the following cycles EXCEPT:

a. binge/intoxication.
b. arousal/incentivization.
c. withdrawal/negative affect.
d. preoccupation/anticipation.

114. Tre's drinking and drug use are motivated by peer approval. As part of the addiction cycle, this represents:

a. impulsivity.
b. compulsivity.
c. negative reinforcement.
d. positive reinforcement.

115. How should the therapist respond to the court's request for a treatment summary?

a. Indicate to the court that the client did not provide signed assent.
b. Send a certified letter to the family requesting payment for services rendered.
c. Take steps to prohibit any disclosure unless a subpoena is issued.
d. Limit the disclosure as narrowly as possible to prevent client harm.

116. An Addictions Professional (AP) provides ongoing treatment for a conservative Muslim female with alcohol use disorder. The client is progressing in individual therapy but continues to have extreme difficulties in her marriage. The AP is a non-Hispanic white male and does not have experience or training in couple therapy. According to the NAADAC Code of Ethics (2021), the AP should FIRST:

a. seek continuing education and training in cultural diversity.
b. provide the client with a culturally-appropriate referral.
c. invite a qualified therapist to participate in treatment.
d. provide the client with online and in-person couple support groups.

117. With regard to co-occurring disorders, what does the term integrated treatment refer to?

a. Meeting both medical and substance use disorder treatment needs
b. Using an eclectic treatment paradigm in the treatment process
c. Incorporating sociocultural issues in the treatment process
d. All-inclusive treatment of mental health and substance use disorders.

118. A woman's initiation of substance use is closely tied to all of the following EXCEPT:

a. a partner or spouse's use.
b. a co-occurring mood disorder.
c. an eating disorder.
d. a personality disorder.

119. Which of the following is NOT a typical stage in the development of cocaine addiction?

a. Compulsive use
b. Experimental use
c. Isolated use
d. Social use

120. What theory is community reinforcement (CR) and contingency management (CM) based upon?

a. Social learning theory
b. Operant conditioning theory
c. Family systems theory
d. Biological-genetic theory

121. There are many approaches and techniques that may be used to help families understand addiction and support sobriety. How does the Bowen family systems theory view the family?

a. An interdependent emotional unit
b. Autonomous members in a collective
c. Functional co-participants in limited endeavors
d. Disparate participants seeking harmony

122. The CAGE questionnaire is a four-question screening tool for which of the following?

a. Cocaine use.
b. Marijuana use.
c. Alcohol use.
d. Opioid use.

123. Using the American Society of Addiction Medicine (ASAM) multidimensional assessment, which dimension measures the client's ability to tolerate and cope with physical discomfort?

a. Recovering/Living environment.
b. Emotional, behavioral, or cognitive conditions and complications.
c. Biomedical conditions and complications.
d. Acute intoxication and/or withdrawal potential.

124. The Substance Abuse and Mental Health Services Administration (SAMHSA) maintains a national registry known as NREPP. What does this acronym refer to?

a. National Registry of Examinations for Psychological Practices
b. National Registry of Excellence in Program Practicum
c. National Registry of Evidence-Based Programs and Practices
d. National Registry of Examiners for Program Procedures

125. Which is NOT true of the Symptom Checklist-90-R (SCL-90-R)?

a. It provides an in-depth assessment of psychopathology.
b. It serves as a means for monitoring treatment progress.
c. It measures symptomatic distress from the past week.
d. It is normed for individuals ages 18 and older.

126. When giving a new client feedback about assessment results, which of these should counselors do first?

a. Ask the client if there were any problems with testing.
b. Encourage the client to ask any questions.
c. Express your appreciation for the client's effort in responding.
d. Ask the client how testing affected perceptions of their substance use.

127. What does the DAP progress note acronym stand for?

a. Description, Assessment, and Progress
b. Details, Assessment, and Progress
c. Documentation, Actions, and Pending
d. Data, Assessment, and Plan

128. Which of the following is NOT a core feature or service that the Center for Substance Abuse Treatment (CSAT) consensus panel agreed upon?

a. Biopsychosocial assessment
b. Individualized treatment planning
c. Case management
d. Recreational therapy

129. Goals for clinical supervision include all of the following EXCEPT:

a. to protect the well-being of clients.
b. to promote professional and ethical practices.
c. to empower the supervisee to grow in their ability to self-supervise.
d. to provide personal and professional support, counseling, and encouragement.

130. What does metabolism do?

a. maintains the composition of the drug
b. alters the composition of the drug
c. alters the drug so it cannot be eliminated from the body
d. maintains the peak intensity of the drug

131. How many levels of treatment placement are recognized by the American Society of Addiction Medicine (ASAM)?

a. Two levels of treatment placement
b. Four levels of treatment placement
c. Six levels of treatment placement
d. Eight levels of treatment placement

132. Using Roberts' seven-stage crisis intervention model, what step must be conducted before exploring a client's feelings and emotions?

a. Formulate a plan of action.
b. Create a follow-up plan.
c. Identify aspects of the crisis or presenting problem.
d. Generate alternative responses.

133. The DSM-5-TR promotes the use of language supporting the notion that race is a social construct. Instead of using race/racial, the DSM-5-TR uses the term:

a. racialized.
b. ethnoracial.
c. racial identity.
d. ethnic minority group.

134. Which one of the following is vital to a comprehensive behavioral health crisis response approach?

a. Increasing reliance on law enforcement to provide crisis assistance.
b. Implementing a crisis response continuum of care.
c. Enhancing communication with crisis counselors to provide seamless entry into the criminal justice system.
d. Providing funding for monetary incentives for individuals who accept medication for OUD.

135. The DSM-5-TR does NOT include withdrawal symptoms for which one of the following?

a. Sedatives.
b. Hallucinogens.
c. Stimulants.
d. Cannabis.

136. Which of the following conditions does alcohol NOT induce?

a. Steatosis
b. Nephrosis
c. Hepatitis
d. Cirrhosis

137. Which one of the following is NOT a component of counselor burnout?

a. Depersonalization.
b. Reduced professional efficacy.
c. Emotional exhaustion.
d. Repeated trauma exposure.

138. What is the case management approach that focuses on helping clients assert direct and personal control in the search for resources?

a. Program of Assertive Community Treatment Model
b. Clinical or Rehabilitation model
c. Brokerage or Generalist Model
d. Strengths-Based Perspective

139. Which is true of the Code of Federal Regulations (CFR) Part 2 regarding the exchange of confidential patient information?

a. It offers patients in federally funded treatment programs protection for general health information.
b. It permits disclosures without patient consent when required for insurance and payment for services.
c. It protects the confidentiality of substance abuse patient records without patient consent.
d. It permits disclosures without consent or court order unless used for medical emergencies or criminal investigations.

140. The first step in relapse prevention begins with assessing situational circumstances, perceptions, and determinants leading to a relapse. Which one of the following cognitive errors occurs when a person blames the relapse on factors beyond their control?

a. Seemingly irrelevant decisions.
b. Abstinence violation effect.
c. Problem of immediate gratification.
d. Covert antecedents.

141. Which of the following involves a counselor adopting a relaxed posture, good eye-contact, and a pleasant tone of voice?

a. attending.
b. empathizing.
c. genuineness.
d. concreteness.

142. Which one of the following refers to the judicious use of available resources?

a. Stewardship.
b. Justice.
c. Candor.
d. Obedience.

143. Psychomotor agitation is a common withdrawal symptom for all of the following substances EXCEPT:

a. alcohol.
b. cannabis.
c. stimulants.
d. sedatives/tranquilizers.

144. Once the NAADAC Ethics Committee determines that a complaint or grievance is valid, potential outcomes include which one of the following?

a. Monetary relief for wrongful conduct.
b. Termination of a member's state licensure or certification.
c. Requests to attend ethics training.
d. Injunctions to temporarily suspend clinical services.

145. Which one of the following alcohol use screening tests is designed specifically for use with adolescents?

a. CAGE
b. CRAFFT
c. MAST
d. AUDIT

146. Compared to men, substance use patterns among women are best reflected in which one of the following statements?

a. Women who use substances are more likely to be diagnosed with bipolar disorder and schizophrenia.
b. Women use smaller amounts for longer durations before developing SUD.
c. Women use substances for a larger variety of reasons.
d. Women are more likely to use all types of illicit substances.

147. How are drugs MOST often removed from the body?

a. through vomit.
b. through exhalation.
c. through urine.
d. through sweat.

148. What is the primary purpose of the Texas Christian University (TCU) Drug Screen 5?

a. To determine the severity of substance use and appropriate level of care.
b. To assess functional domains and develop treatment goals.
c. To evaluate dangerousness and risk taking in substance use patterns.
d. To correlate substance use patterns with emerging behavioral health concerns.

149. Guiding principles in treatment planning are identified by which acronym?

a. MTSRA
b. MATRS
c. MSRTA
d. MRAST

150. Of the following statements, which one is NOT true of cirrhosis?

a. Few symptoms are present until its advanced stages.
b. Cirrhosis can be caused by hepatitis B and C.
c. Treating underlying conditions can reverse cirrhosis.
d. Obesity is a risk factor for developing cirrhosis.

Answer Key and Explanations for Test #1

1. C: Cannabis use disorder is associated with developing higher instances of schizophrenia. This is particularly true for young males. Heavy marijuana use can induce or worsen symptoms of schizophrenia. It is also associated with early onset of schizophrenia among individuals who are genetically predisposed. Substance use disorder (SUD) often co-occurs with PTSD, obsessive-compulsive disorder, and attention deficit hyperactivity disorder; however, cannabis use disorder is more commonly associated with inducing higher instances of schizophrenia.

2. C: Opium, caffeine, and nicotine are all psychoactive substances because they effect in individual's behavior and mood. The most active ingredient in opium is morphine, which carries the potential for tolerance, dependence, and withdrawal. Opium is a central nervous system depressant, while caffeine and nicotine are central nervous system stimulants. Aspirin is a pain killer, but does not have psychoactive properties,

3. C: Ask, advise, assess, assist, and arrange. The "Smoking Cessation Practice Guidelines" recommend: 1) ask regarding tobacco use (as a rule, a pack or more a day indicates a strong addiction); 2) advise smoking cessation in a "strong and personalized manner," describing the risks and health benefits involved and clarifying that tobacco in any form is not safe; 3) assess a client's willingness to stop in the next 30 days and provide resource materials; motivation may include keeping a log, writing down pros and cons, encouraging tapering back, etc.; 4) assist with nonconfrontational counsel, mobilization of social support, and pharmacotherapy referral if appropriate; and 5) arrange to assess the individual's use in subsequent follow-up. Effective support includes: multiple therapeutic sessions; offering training in problem-solving and coping; bolstering social support, including a smoking cessation support group; reminders that many attempts are often required; pointing out excusive defenses (e.g., rationalization, denial), and identification of fears in quitting.

4. A: The primary focus of Leon's screening for cannabis use is to determine whether he is at risk for or currently has use-related problems. With positive screenings, additional evaluations and assessments are used to determine if the severity of use or withdrawal symptoms warrant immediate attention or require an alternate treatment setting. Risk and protective factors are identified during the clinical interview or biopsychosocial assessment.

5. C: The counselor uses the Cannabis Use Disorder Identification Test-Revised (CUDIT-R), which has questions similar to the Alcohol Use Disorders Identification Test (AUDIT), but it is instead used to measure cannabis use. The CUDIT-R uses cutoff scores to identify those at risk for developing cannabis use disorder (CUD) (i.e., sensitivity) and those who do not meet the criteria (i.e., specificity). The Drug Abuse Screening Test-10 (DAST-10) is a 10-question instrument assessing the effects and consequences of various substances. The Posttraumatic Stress Disorder Checklist (PCL)-5 measures symptoms of PTSD, while the Severity of Dependence Scale (SDS) measures the person's degrees of dependence on cannabis and other substances within the past year.

6. C: The combination of cannabis and alcohol produces an additive effect, meaning that the effects produced are the sum of each individual substance. This differs from an antagonistic effect in that the combination of substances decreases their effects. The potentiation, or synergistic, effect occurs when the combination of substances creates a reaction greater than what each individual substance produces.

7. D: The DSM-5-TR uses the total number of identified symptoms (out of 11) to specify whether one's cannabis use disorder (CUD) is mild, moderate, or severe. Mild CUD is indicated by 2 or 3 symptoms, moderate CUD requires 4 or 5 symptoms to be present, and severe CUD is marked by 6 or more symptoms. Categories or domains for each symptom include impaired control, social impairment, risky use, and physical dependence.

8. B: Doctor shopping is closely associated with substance misuse. Substance misuse occurs when legal substances such as prescription pills are misused, for example, by using more medication than prescribed, altering administration routes, and taking medication prescribed to another person. Substance use broadly covers all psychoactive drugs and other illicit substances known to alter perceptions. Substance dependency occurs when individuals continue to use drugs or alcohol despite significant problems in functioning, with brain alterations resulting in cravings, tolerance, and withdrawal. The terms substance addiction and substance dependency are used interchangeably by some experts, noting shared traits, such as psychological and/or physical dependence, whereas others use the term addiction when referring to behavioral addiction (e.g., gambling disorder). The National Institute on Drug Abuse describes addiction as compulsive drug seeking behavior despite suffering harmful consequences.

9. A: The 5 Ps is an integrative screening instrument for pregnant people that assesses for drug and alcohol use for a pregnant person's parents, peers, and partner. It also assesses for pregnancy use and past use. For individuals determined to be of high risk, two additional questions are asked regarding the use of opioids, narcotics, or pain medications in the past year and whether they were prescribed. The Substance Use Brief Screen is a prescreening instrument for all individuals that asks, "How many times in the past year have you used a recreational drug or a prescription medication for nonmedical reasons?" The CRAFFT (which stands for car, relax, alone, forget, family or friends, trouble) instrument measures substance use in individuals younger than age 21. The Tobacco, Alcohol, Prescription Medication, and Other Substance Use (TAPS) tool is composed of TAPS-1 and TAPS-2 questions for use with all populations. If a client's score on the TAPS-1 tool is greater than "never," then the TAPS-2 tool is administered.

10. A: Psychoactive drugs are drugs that alter mood, awareness, behavior, and thoughts. Categories of psychoactive drugs include depressants, stimulants, opiates, and hallucinogens.

11. B: Several mandatory disclosures must be provided during informed consent, including informing clients of their right to refuse services (i.e., client autonomy), confidentiality and its limitations including duty to warn, and information about billing procedures including fees and nonpayment policies. Principle I-3 of the NAADAC Code of Ethics (2021) states that mandatory disclosures must include "an explicit explanation as to the nature of all services to be provided and methodologies and theories typically utilized, purposes, goals, techniques, procedures, limitations, potential risks, and benefits of services."

12. C: A urine drug screen confirms the detection of drug metabolites. This test cannot determine the amount of substance used, nor can it determine the substances used throughout a person's lifetime. Most urine drug screens use an immunoassay drug test panel, which is highly sensitive but has low specificity, which can lead to false positives. For this reason, the two-step approach is commonly used. If a person tests positive on an immunoassay screen, it is followed by confirmatory gas chromatography-mass spectrometry screen, which is high in specificity.

13. C: The Addiction Severity Index (ASI) was first released in 1977 and formally adopted for use by the National Institute on Drug Abuse in 1980. The ASI was developed by the Drug Evaluation Network Systems, which was sponsored in this endeavor by the White House Office of National

Drug Control Policy (ONDCP) and the Center for Substance Abuse Treatment (CSAT). Since that time, the ASI has become the most widely used assessment instrument in the field of addictions. It is recommended as a baseline instrument for addiction assessment by a great many governmental and private substance abuse treatment organizations, and due to its standardized questions, it is particularly useful for research. A teen version (T-ASI) and a shortened version (ASI-Lite) are also available. Currently in its fifth iteration, version six is in development.

14. C: The pioneering University of California, Los Angeles (UCLA) nonverbal communication researcher Albert Mehrabian has revealed that approximately 50 percent of all communication is exchanged nonverbally in the form of body language. According to Mehrabian, there are three fundamental elements in face-to-face communication: (1) the actual words used; (2) the tone of voice used; and (3) nonverbal behaviors (e.g., facial expression, body posture, gestures). If the nonverbal elements are incongruent, the behavior and tonality tend to be seen as more genuine than any words expressed. Given the importance of genuine compassion and empathy in the therapeutic process, body language is particularly important. To optimize nonverbal communication, the counselor should be seated two to four feet from the client, with no intervening barrier (e.g., a desk), leaning forward, legs and arms uncrossed, hands open, nodding to communications expressed, and making direct eye contact (if cultural permits it). The client's body movements (including micro-movements, such as nostril flaring or quivering chin) should be noted and responded to appropriately.

15. B: Principle I-11 of the NAADAC Code of Ethics (2021) states that APs must try to avoid dual, or multiple, relationships with clients. If such relationships are unavoidable, APs take appropriate precautions, including obtaining consent, seeking supervision or consultation, and documenting recommendations. The duty to warn does not apply to multiple relationships. Instead, duty to warn is the obligation to warn or protect individuals at risk of imminent harm due to a client's actions or inactions.

16. C: Principle II-1 of the NAADAC Code of Ethics (2021) states that clients receiving multidisciplinary care have the right to ask who their team members are and what information is being exchanged. Multidisciplinary teams include case managers, psychiatrists, additional medical professionals (e.g., pharmacists, nurse practitioners), social workers, counselors, family therapists, and psychologists. Clients are required to sign authorizations for each team member permitting multidisciplinary consultations.

17. B: Boundary violations consist of dual relationships that are exploitative. Dual, or multiple, relationships refer to circumstances that place the client and counselor in more than one role. Not all dual relationships are boundary violations. Boundary violations occur when there is a power differential between the role of counselor and client. Elements of boundary violations include exploitation, manipulation, coercion, and/or deception. Examples of boundary violations include sexual or business relationships between the client and counselor. Boundary crossings are dual relationships that deviate from the professional relationship between the client and counselor. Boundary crossings may be unavoidable, unintentional, or therapeutic (e.g., bartering, nonsexual hugs, extending sessions for clients in crisis).

18. B: A discharge summary encompasses: (1) client demographics and general profile; (2) symptoms at admission; (3) interventions provided and outcomes realized; (4) critical incidents that occurred and resolution processes for each; (5) treatment goal progress and obstacles to progress; and (6) recommendations for further treatment in light of all treatment program events and progress. A continuing care plan encompasses: (1) options based on client's successes and residual needs; (2) appropriate resource linkages (food, housing, education, family needs, and legal issues); and (3) schedules for group meetings, twelve-step programs, and counseling, as well as other interventions. The discharge summary depicts what was done, why, and outcomes, as well as future recommendations. A continuing care plan explores options, identifies resources of benefit, and serves to schedule and coordinate all aftercare meetings and services.

19. B: Consequently, this group tends to delay treatment, which leads to less care overall. Deference to parents and the need to sustain family pride are at times problematic variables. Religious ceremonies and traditional celebrations are central cultural components, and alcohol use is typically expected at such events. On average, 40 percent of this group report alcohol use, and 5 percent report illicit substance use, with the highest rates among Puerto Ricans and the lowest among Cubans. Spanish-language groups and counselors are important contributions to the treatment process. Locating Spanish-speaking twelve-step groups can also make a substantial difference to positive, long-term outcomes.

20. B: The Adult Substance Abuse Subtle Screening Inventory – 4 (SASSI-4) is composed of both obvious and subtle, making it useful in situations where individuals are either unwilling or unable to acknowledge substance abuse problems. The Michigan Alcohol Screening Test (MAST) is one of the oldest and most accurate alcohol screening tests available, but it offers no special tools for ferreting out issues of truth. The Screening, Brief Intervention, and Referral to Treatment (SBIRT) is a quick and simple tool for identifying those who use substances at at-risk levels and those already experiencing substance use issues. However, it offers no special tools for circumventing compromised truth telling. The Addiction Severity Index (ASI) is not a screening tool but a tool for assessment and treatment planning.

21. C: Common reasons for youths initiating substance use include the belief they will gain peer support; have a pleasurable experience; and/or have improved work, school, or sports performance. Individuals initiating substance use may disbelieve that they will have adverse consequences, but this is often neither a deterrent nor a motivating factor.

22. B: In addition to inhalants, Tyler states that his bullies held him down and made him take MDMA, (aka Molly or ecstasy).

23. D: Bullying is intentional aggression that is unwanted, harmful, and often repeated. Bullying can be indirect, as in cases involving gossip or instances that occur online. There are contextual dimensions of bullying, including the family environment, school climate, and community setting, which are significant when targeting prevention and intervention services. Bullying is relational in that it can potentially destroy reputations or damage relationships. This can occur through gossiping, ignoring, or engaging in harmful electronic messaging (e.g., posting embarrassing photos without consent). Youths who experience bullying are at risk for developing SUD, mental disorders, and other physical health conditions.

24. A: Inhalants from whipped cream propellant canisters (whippets) contain nitrous oxide gases. Nitrites are found in leather cleaners, room deodorizers, and chest pain medications. Examples include cyclohexyl nitrate (i.e., poppers) and isoamyl (amyl) and isobutyl (butyl) nitrite (i.e., snappers, Quick Silver). Aerosols are sprays containing solvents and propellants such as fluorocarbon and butane. Volatile solvents are liquid substances that change to gas (i.e., vaporize) at room temperature and can be found in mothballs, felt-tip markers, lighter fluid, and glue.

25. A: The DSM-5-TR uses the number of symptoms present to determine the severity of substance use disorder (SUD). Of the 11 symptoms or criteria for SUD, guidelines for severity include (1) mild, which is indicated by the presence of 2 or 3 symptoms; (2) moderate, which is indicated by the presence of 4 or 5 symptoms; and (3) severe, which is assigned to individuals with 6 or more symptoms. The 11 criteria for SUD are categorized into four groups: physical dependence, risky use, social problems, and impaired control. Although specific criteria address functional impairment, substance-related consequences, withdrawal, or dependence, the subtotal of all criteria determines the severity.

26. D: Sudden sniffing death is caused by heart failure, with an increased risk among individuals engaging in long-session use (i.e., inhaling the substance for a long duration). Commonly implicated chemicals are in aerosols, propane, and butane. These substances are commonly inhaled or huffed. Inhalant use deprives the body of oxygen, with is required for the heart to function. Heart failure and death can occur almost immediately and result from one or multiple uses.

27. B: The client is likely to be in the maintenance stage of change. The stages of readiness to change are precontemplation, contemplation, preparation, action, and maintenance. Working with the client on relapse prevention is most applicable to the maintenance stage, wherein the client has remained sober but must make continuing efforts to consolidate gains. The client also struggles with clinical depression. Despite persistent depressive symptoms, precipitating factors are unknown. Assuming the client attends therapy to address those symptoms, it can be assumed that the client is either in the action or maintenance stage. The remaining stages of change include: (1) precontemplation: In this stage there is a total or partial lack of awareness regarding behaviors requiring change; (2) contemplation: clients in this stage are aware of behaviors requiring change but remain ambivalent; (3) preparation: in this stage, clients examine how life will look if a change is made. Plans are made to change in the near future; (4) action: clients begin to make necessary changes. Some practitioners also include relapse or termination in the stages of change model.

28. B: About half of individuals who experience a seizure during alcohol withdrawal will develop delirium tremens. Delirium tremens, which can last up to 1 week or longer, is the most severe complication of alcohol withdrawal, with symptoms including, but not limited to, hallucinations, restlessness, tachycardia, electrolyte imbalance, hyperthermia, and confusion. Hyperreflexia, or overly responsive bodily reflexes (e.g., spasms, twitching), is a mild symptom of alcohol withdrawal. Anhedonia is the loss of pleasure that can be experienced in various stages of alcohol withdrawal. Insomnia is a mild symptom of alcohol withdrawal.

29. D: From the first therapeutic community (Synanon, founded in 1958 in California by Chuck Dederich), treatment communities (TCs) were organized as controlled, drug-free residential treatment settings providing intensive and comprehensive treatment. The central goal is to produce a holistically healthy lifestyle, engaging emotional, psychological, and social issues that may lead to substance use. Residents learn from each other, staff members, and other authority figures. This has come to be referred to as community-as-method perspective, which sees the whole community (clients, staff, social structure, and daily activities) as the active therapeutic agent. The TC model has been expanded to include additional services, such as mental health and medical services, educational and vocational services, and family education and therapy. Today, many TC programs are carried out in intensive outpatient treatment (IOT) programs, serving clients transitioning out of residential or incarceration settings or bypassing residential treatment altogether.

30. B: The Substance Use Brief Screen is a four-item screening tool for unhealthy use of tobacco, alcohol, illicit substances, and prescription drugs. The Addiction Severity Index consists of 11 questions measuring the effects and severity of substance use in several areas of client functioning. The Drug Abuse Screening Test-10 is a 10-question instrument assessing the effects of various classes of drugs but excludes alcohol and tobacco. The Screening to Brief Intervention targets adolescent substance use for tobacco, alcohol, marijuana, prescription drugs, inhalants, and K2/spice.

31. B: Social determinants of health (SDOHs) contribute to behavioral health disparities among diverse populations. SDOHs refer to the conditions in which a person lives, grows, learns, and works. Examples of SDOHs include but are not limited to education, social support, socioeconomic status, and access to health care. SDOHs are influenced by societal structures and categorizations of individuals into social strata, with inequitable resources allocated to those who are not in power. Whereas individual health choices contribute to poorer health outcomes, inequities caused by SDOHs are the drivers of behavioral health disparities among diverse groups. The belief that disparities are caused by a lack of perseverance or the misuse of equally distributed resources is inaccurate. These beliefs reinforce the stigma associated with behavioral health in underserved populations.

32. D: The NAADAC Ethics Committee can accept complaints or grievances against an AP who fails to use evidence-based practices. The NAADAC Ethics Committee cannot take anonymous complaints, civil cases involving billing or financial restitution, and complaints against a business's policies and procedures. The committee can only respond to complaints against members of the NAADAC and/or individuals or businesses certified by the National Certification Commission for Addiction Professionals. The committee can respond to violations of federal, local, and state laws, violations of the NAADAC Code of Ethics principles, and any circumstance involving client harm or risk for harm. Complaints involving an NAADAC member's credentials or licensure must first be submitted to the state. The committee then makes its determination after considering the state's findings.

33. B: The Four Quadrants Model is a classification model for co-occurring disorders that uses symptom severity to determine the client's level of care and treatment setting. The client's clinical diagnosis is not considered. The four quadrants are categorized as follows: (I) less severe mental disorder/less severe SUD, (II) more severe mental disorder/less severe SUD, (III) less severe mental disorder/more severe SUD, and (IV) more severe mental disorder/more severe SUD.

34. B: Approximately 50% of individuals who experience seizures from alcohol withdrawal go on to experience delirium tremens.

35. D: Because John's use of yoga and meditation are integrated with other therapies, they are considered complementary. If yoga and meditation were the only forms of treatment John received, they would be classified as alternative treatments. Behavioral treatment focuses on changing behaviors related to substance use or co-occurring issues. Examples include cognitive behavioral therapy, motivational enhancement therapy, and brief intervention. Conventional medicine is also known as modernized or Westernized treatment. This form of treatment is used to eliminate disease and underlying symptoms based on what works with a majority of the population. Conventional medicine is less likely to take into account individual or cultural differences.

36. C: John is prescribed disulfiram, which causes unpleasant symptoms (e.g., vomiting, flushing) when the user is drinking by blocking the metabolism of alcohol. Naltrexone and acamprosate are also FDA-approved medications for AUD. Naltrexone is effective for moderate to severe symptoms of AUD and does not require abstinence from alcohol to begin treatment. For individuals with contraindications to naltrexone, acamprosate, an FDA-approved medication for AUD, is recommended. Acamprosate decreases cravings or urges and helps individuals with AUD maintain abstinence.

37. A: Buprenorphine is used to treat opioid use disorder. Methadone and naltrexone are also FDA-approved treatment for opioid use disorder. FDA-approved medication for alcohol use disorder includes acamprosate, disulfiram, and naltrexone. Topiramate is used to treat migraine headaches and seizures. While not FDA-approved to treat addictive disorders, topiramate is sometimes used off-label to treat heavy drinking and binge-eating disorders.

38. C: Culture is best understood broadly, referring to a shared set of values, norms, and beliefs common to any group of people, whether it is based on race, ethnicity, sexual orientation, ability, gender identity, religion, economic status, nationality, age, or any other shared identity or affiliation.

39. D: The Centers for Disease Control and Prevention describes adverse childhood experiences (ACEs) as "potentially traumatic events" occurring before a child's 18th birthday." ACEs include child abuse and neglect, witnessing violence, and parental abandonment or separation. ACEs also include any event that impacts a child's emotional well-being and their sense of safety and security. ACEs are linked to chronic behavioral health difficulties, with higher scores on the ACEs Questionnaire indicating the potential for long-term adverse consequences.

40. D: Research indicates that ACEs Questionnaire scores are highest among males, racialized populations, and individuals who are unemployed. Children with younger parents are at a higher risk for ACEs.

41. A: The cumulative toll of ACEs produces toxic stress, leading to physical, social, emotional, and mental impairments. Toxic stress is the body's response to excessive, prolonged, and chronic stressors experienced in the absence of a supportive caregiver. Positive stress responses are natural reactions to anxiety or stress, producing mild increases in heart rate and hormone levels. Neurological stress responses involve the sympathetic nervous system, which is responsible for fight-or-flight reactions, and the parasympathetic nervous system, which helps the body rest and digest as a person recovers from a stressful event. Tolerable stress occurs when a child's stressful encounters are mitigated by a supportive and calming caregiver, allowing the child's body to recover and return to its natural state.

42. C: Developing discrepancy is accomplished by examining differences between the client's values and behaviors. In this scenario, the counselor could discuss the differences between Fran's drug and alcohol use and her value as a surrogate parent. Motivational enhancement therapy also emphasizes change talk over sustain talk, reframes resistance as a normal part of change, and promotes the use of affirmations, along with open questions, reflections, and summarizations.

43. B: Life-threatening withdrawal symptoms, including respiratory distress, coma, and death, can occur with alcohol, opioids, and sedatives. Cocaine overdose, rather than withdrawal, is implicated in one out of five overdose deaths. Cocaine toxicity can result in cardiovascular complications, stroke, and death.

44. C: Authoritative parenting is least likely to serve as a risk factor for developing SUD. Parents exhibiting an authoritative parenting style implement age-appropriate rules and consequences, take advantage of teachable moments, promote self-efficacy, and provide children with consistency and structure. Research shows that uninvolved, authoritarian, and permissive parenting styles increase children's SUD risk. Uninvolved parents show little warmth or interest in their children, whereas authoritarian parents are overly strict and punitive. Permissive parents may show warmth and interest but lack discipline and structure. They may also resort to bribing their children to behave.

45. B: A family risk factor for developing AUD is having parents who are both full-time employees. With both parents working, they may be unavailable to their children, leading to little supervision and less time spent monitoring alcohol use. Protective factors, or characteristics that decrease the likelihood of developing AUD, include family cohesion (i.e., togetherness), having adequate socioeconomic resources, and secure attachment.

46. B: Zoe's help-seeking behavior is a protective factor. Zoe desires to be a better parent and seeks help regardless of the stigma associated with intergenerational substance use. Protective factors decrease the likelihood of developing SUD. Zoe describes her parenting style as strict with little structure and consistency, making it a potential risk factor. Jack's temperament is reflected by nightly temper tantrums and an inability to self-regulate, which would also serve as a risk factor. Lastly, Jack's school readiness would not be a protective factor because he experiences cognitive and language delays.

47. D: The family environment is an example of a proximal risk factor for developing SUD. Substance abuse prevention in early childhood is based on the overarching principle that prevention can positively affect the lifetime course for developing SUD. The context for prevention and intervention includes proximal factors or the child's immediate environment (e.g., family, school). Distal risk factors for the development of SUD include genetics, temperament, and family history. Distal factors are risk factors that indicate an underlying vulnerability or likelihood of developing SUD in the future.

48. C: Risk factors for contracting hepatitis C virus include having HIV, hepatitis B, and fatty liver disease. It affects more men than women, and alcohol use has been shown to worsen symptoms and has a greater risk of infection.

49. A: The AP must obtain informed consent and releases of information prior to recording. If a clinician desires to record a session, the client must be informed of the purpose of the recording, as well as the policies related to access, storage, and disposal of the recording. A release of information must be obtained and signed to allow 3rd party observations.

50. C: Research indicates that shorter wait times (i.e., access to services) for initial intake appointments are positively correlated with lower dropout rates and improved client outcomes. In some cases, client autonomy, or the freedom to choose one's own destiny, may also be enhanced.

51. C: Principle VI-4 of the NAADAC Code of Ethics (2021) outlines the execution of informed consent to include but not be limited to social media policy, emergency protocols, and procedures for when the AP is unavailable. Additionally, response times for asynchronous (e.g., email, faxed documents) rather than synchronous communication (e.g., teletherapy, instant messages) must also be reviewed.

52. B: In-person counseling is superior to e-therapy for upholding and maintaining confidentiality. There are more significant risks with e-therapy, including but not limited to the use, storage, transmission, and disposal of confidential client records. An AP's ability to assert privilege, uphold standards of practice, and adhere to professional responsibilities is the same for in-person and e-therapy services.

53. A: The AP's response is an example of an affirmation. Zia expresses feeling hesitant and embarrassed when scheduling her initial appointment. The AP responds by stating, "It took a lot of courage for you to follow through with the appointment. That's a big first step!" This affirms Zia's ability to move in the direction of change. Reflections are counselor responses that show accurate interpretations of a client's verbal and nonverbal messages. Clarification expresses a counselor's attempt to accurately understand a client's experiences. Empathy is the ability of counselors to put themselves in the shoes of their clients and to understand the feelings associated with their experiences.

54. C: Principle II-19 of the NAADAC Code of Ethics (2021) states that before videotaping an e-therapy session, the AP must first obtain informed consent and releases of information permitting third-party observation. Informed consent may include the following: a review of confidentiality; use of a virtual private network and other digital practices; supervisory approval; crisis protocols; and methods used to store, transfer, and dispose of client data. APs must maintain compliance with HIPAA and 42 CFR Part 2, but preapproval is not required. However, providers must have a signed business associate agreement with virtual private network providers to ensure HIPAA compliance.

55. C: The sedative effects of alcohol are caused by activation of the primary inhibitory neurotransmitter known as gamma-aminobutyric acid (GABA). Alcohol acts as a central nervous system (CNS) depressant by enhancing the activity of GABA receptors. This occurs during alcohol use, with protracted use decreasing GABA activity and abrupt cessation resulting in GABA overactivity. Substances that increase CNS activity, such as stimulants, release catecholamines, including epinephrine, norepinephrine, and dopamine. Hallucinogens affect the parasympathetic nervous system, whose primary neurotransmitter is acetylcholine. Acetylcholine is responsible for memory, attention, and mood.

56. D: Screening is the process in which a client's eligibility for a treatment program or intervention is identified. Counselors use screening to determine appropriate client care and seek to match clients with available community resources. Evaluations and assessments differ from screenings in that they are more comprehensive and are commonly designed to provide a comprehensive case conceptualization, diagnosis, and treatment plan. Screenings, evaluations, and assessments often lead to referrals to appropriate programs.

57. D: As outlined in Principle I-40 of the NAADAC Code of Ethics (2021), APs must obtain supervision or consultation and document recommendations before accepting or declining gifts from clients. Principle I-40 also states that "providers shall take into account the therapeutic relationship, the monetary value of the gift, the client's motivation for giving the gift, and the counselor's motivation for wanting to accept or decline the gift." It is a best practice to consider the cultural implications associated with gift giving; however, this is not included in Principle I-40.

58. D: Confidentiality is best reviewed at the beginning of the research study. Principle IX-4 of the NAADAC Code of Ethics (2021) states that researchers must comply with state, local, and federal policies regarding confidentiality. APs must also adhere to institutional and agency practices and guidelines and convey to research participants that information obtained during the study will be confidential. During the study, APs may need to reiterate their adherence to confidentiality and instances requiring mandatory disclosures; however, this occurs on an ongoing basis rather than at predetermined intervals. Although APs remain open and willing to clarify issues regarding confidentiality, the need to do so rests with the AP rather than the client. Confidentiality reviews are conducted at the counselor's (rather than the client's) discretion. Confidentiality is also emphasized during debriefing but is best reviewed at the beginning of the research study.

59. D: APs conducting anonymous research studies are ethically responsible for protecting the anonymity of participants by refraining from collecting personal identifiers that would directly or indirectly link responses to a specific participant. Researchers must protect the integrity of studies by honoring anonymity, confidentiality, and privacy. Privacy is protected when researchers collect only essential information. Confidentiality is upheld by protecting a research subject's identifiable data and unauthorized access to research data.

60. C: According to IX-13 of the NAADAC Code of Ethics (2021), deception is only permissible if it is essential to the research protocol and is approved by an institutional review board or human subjects committee. Additionally, APs must obtain informed consent and ensure that research protocols are followed, confidentiality is upheld, and participants are not subject to coercion.

61. B: If the ethical complaint with NAADAC is found to be valid against Max, this may result in revocation of his NAADAC membership, requests for him to attend ethics training, or dismissal of the case if malpractice cannot be proven. Terminating a provider's certification or licensure is not within the NAADAC Ethics Committee's purview.

62. B: Assessment is designed to obtain valuable information for formulating a clinical diagnosis and determining the direction of treatment. Assessment is an ongoing, comprehensive examination of a client's background and history, including the influence of biological, psychological, social, and spiritual factors. This process helps determine the presence of SUD and any co-occurring disorders. Orientation occurs once a person is screened and undergoes an intake. Orientation is the process of disclosing unique aspects of the treatment program to the client, including payment for services, ethical considerations, and what services are available to the client. Screening helps establish a client's appropriateness to a specific program. It is the first phase in determining if the client is using drugs and/or alcohol and to what degree of severity.

63. C: Motivational interviewing is an evidence-based practice based on the work of Prochaska and DiClemente's Stages of Change model. Addiction professionals (APs) use motivational interviewing to communicate to clients that they are not simply helping the client but also helping the client begin to help themselves. The AP accomplishes this by employing basic interaction techniques (OARS):O: Open-ended questions are used to help the client reflect on their story and perception of their substance use; A: Affirmation of strengths and validation of the client's internal motivation; R: Reflective listening, which involves displaying empathy and unconditional positive regard; S: Summarization of session content. This can be done throughout the session or as a way to wrap up each session.

64. B: The case management clinical or rehabilitation approaches integrate clinical therapy and resource activities together. Both needs are met by the case manager rather than separate providers. Researchers have posited that it is not feasible or functional to divide these two activities for an extended time. To this end, the Clinical or Rehabilitation model merges these two activities by training case managers to see beyond solely environmental issues to other client-focused needs. To this end, the case manager is positioned to provide psychotherapeutic services, offer family therapy, and teach essential skills in a variety of areas, including relapse prevention, and so on. Beyond the usual repertoire of case management functions (assessment, planning, linkage, monitoring, and advocacy [per the Joint Commission on Accreditation of Healthcare Organizations] or assessing, arranging, coordinating, monitoring, evaluating, and advocacy [per the National Association of Social Workers]), the case manager should also address issues of transference, countertransference, client internalizations of observations, theories of ego functioning, and so on. In this way the client's needs can be met in a more holistic and integrated fashion, which should lead to enhanced outcomes.

65. C: Certified Alcohol and Drug Abuse Counselors (CADC), absent additional mental health training and licensure, do not have the credentials and training necessary to diagnose mental disorders. CADC's are well within their scope of practice to screen, assess, and otherwise evaluate clients for substance abuse issues and to formulate and carry out substance abuse treatment plans. Because of the frequency with which co-occurring mental disorders, CADCs can become very familiar and proficient with numerous commonly occurring mental disorders. It can therefore seem natural to broaden the scope of practice as experience grows. However, legal scope-of-practice parameters do not provide for CADCs to diagnose mental disorders, and it is essential that they receive appropriate training, supervision, or consultation regarding the diagnosis and treatment of individuals with co-occurring disorders.

66. A: Counselors working with clients in crisis must differentiate between substance-induced disorders and independent (i.e., singular) mood disorders because suicide rates are highest among those with independent mood disorders. Pharmacological treatment is recommended for substance-induced disorders and independent disorders, with antidepressants recommended for depressive symptoms and antipsychotics for manic episodes. Although medically monitored withdrawal may be necessary for some individuals with a substance-induced mood disorder, it is not necessary for all individuals because intoxication or withdrawal serves as an onset specifier. Lastly, collateral support is essential for all clients in crisis, with both disorders characterized by symptoms that include depressed mood, suicidal ideation, anhedonia, and feelings of worthlessness.

67. B: These feelings can arise out of the counselor's past, or they can emerge in reaction to transference issues brought into the counselor-client relationship by the client. Unhealthy countertransference occurs when unresolved problems and feelings are projected onto the client. Absent clear boundaries and careful self-awareness, the counselor can lose the objectivity necessary to meet the client's needs and understand emerging issues. Countertransference is not the same as reacting to clear presentations from the client (e.g., positively when the client is pleasant and responsive and negatively if the client has a difficult personality). Diligent self-awareness can help the counselor identify the source of feelings along with the nature of the feelings and can help the counselor better serve the client, who may be evoking similar feelings and many others. When client needs and countertransference run together, the counselor may uncover past issues prematurely and thereby compromise the client's welfare.

68. B: Not all mental health conditions require long-term pharmacotherapy. In some cases, traditional pharmacotherapy may involve the use of dependency-producing medications that may not be appropriate for certain individuals. However, most individuals with co-occurring substance abuse and mental health disorders can receive well-chosen medications appropriate to their conditions. It is important not to rule out medication therapy out of hand as untreated mental health conditions can contribute greatly to substance abuse relapse. This can occur both in an effort to self-medicate and because untreated mental health problems can reduce otherwise adequate defenses against a return to substance abuse. Consequently, mutual-help groups have become more amenable to the use of necessary psychiatric medications.

69. C: Attachment theory provides a theoretical framework for understanding the consequences of parental substance use and unresponsive parenting. Inconsistent or unresponsive parenting fails to meet a child's need for security and safety. Children in the early childhood stage of development are increasingly vulnerable to the impact of neglectful parenting. The consequences of unhealthy attachment include increased vulnerability to trauma, stress reactions, anxiety, depression, poor boundaries, and intergenerational transmission of substance use. Change theory uses a biopsychosocial approach and is based on Prochaska & DiClemente's Transtheoretical Model of the Stages of Change. Behavioral theory could be applied to parenting styles based on operant conditioning, reinforcement, or punishment; however, it does not account for the child's need for healthy attachments and the resulting social, emotional, mental, and behavioral manifestations.

Circular communications theory is an interpersonal theory based on the bidirectional encoding of reciprocal messaging.

70. A: Dimension 4 of the ASAM multidimensional assessment, "Readiness to change," incorporates the transtheoretical model of behavioral change (aka the stages of change model). Developed by Prochaska and DiClemente in the late 1970s, the transtheoretical model is based on theoretical models of motivation and behavioral change and includes the following stages: precontemplation, contemplation, preparation, action, and maintenance. The ASAM Criteria Assessment Interview Guide encourages examiners to remember that clients are often in the action stage in at least one area of functioning and stresses the importance of assessing client insight or interest in learning more about substance use.

71. A: During the annual evaluation, two key elements of evaluation are process and outcome. Process follows: drug testing results, individual or group interventions offered (session attendance, topics covered, etc.), and treatment plan formulation rationale and modifications. Each area covered is eventually aggregated into a total agency intervention and success or efficacy scores. Outcome addresses primary program goals and the level of success realized for each. Key indices include: attainment and maintenance of sobriety, educational or vocational goals, progress in behavioral goals, and degrees of success in family and social goals. Documentation (or charting) involves recording treatment interventions, together with levels of success, challenges, and the type and rationale for any modifications in interventions, goals, and success measures. Current law prevents recording human immunodeficiency virus (HIV) status in a regular chart, and counselors should avoid recording information that might be used to penalize or harm a client, should law enforcement discover or obtain the record.

72. A: When compared to their male counterparts, females ages 12–21 who drink alcohol have higher instances of alcohol-related blackouts, liver cancer, and heart disease. Males in all age cohorts have higher rates of alcohol-related deaths and emergency department visits.

73. A: The best description of a drug is a substance taken for a desired biological effect. Drugs can be pharmacological or psychoactive. Pharmacological drugs are taken for health-related benefits, while psychoactive drugs are often used alter behavior and/or mood. Not all drugs are harmful nor addictive.

74. D: Programmed confrontation is a method used to mobilize a substance user (typically a husband) to accept treatment. It is carried out by a family member (typically a wife). To effectively engage programmed confrontation, the family member receives training in Unilateral Family Therapy (UFT). The training is conducted over a period of months, covering important issues such as personal coping (with the addict's abuse), helping him or her cut back on substance use, and ways to encourage treatment acceptance. By the fifth month, the addict is typically prepared. UFT was influenced by the community reinforcement approach (CRA), and the Johnson Intervention. The Johnson Intervention utilizes family mobilization, coaching, and rehearsing to motivate a potential client into treatment—usually using an element of surprise. The model focuses on the addict's positive traits and the negative changes that result from addiction. Specific examples of behavior issues are presented in a loving, caring manner to break through the addict's denial and encourage treatment. The UFT success rate is 37 percent entering treatment, compared to 11 percent where no UFT techniques were involved.

75. C: The ask-tell-ask technique is exemplified by: "Can you explain what we've discussed." The "ask-tell-ask" technique, also known as the "teach back" technique" is effective for client engagement and demands that the provider shifts from a directive approach (i.e., telling the client what to do) to a collaborative approach (i.e., insuring understanding and partnership). This collaborative approach works by asking open-ended and goal-oriented questions. Simple "yes" or "no" questions can impede understanding and effectiveness. While "Can you explain what we have discussed?" is open-ended, it is goal-oriented in that the provider can then instruct the client to explain or the provider can offer a clearer explanation. This process helps build the therapeutic alliance and establish treatment plan goals.

76. C: According to the 2021 National Survey on Drug Use and Health, American Indian or Alaska Native people account for nearly 28% of individuals diagnosed with SUD, individuals who are black and African American make up 17.2%, white individuals make up 17%, and Hispanic or Latino individuals account for 15.7%.

77. A: A genogram is a family relationship map that utilizes special symbols to trace consanguineous relationships, major events, and family dynamics over multiple generations. Genograms are often used to identify patterns of mental and physical illnesses, including issues of addiction. A genogram is dynamic as it is revised as often as new information is discovered. Genograms can also be created for a family of choice (nonbiological relationships, such as spouses, significant others, friends, etc.) from which similar patterns can be derived. Another mapping tool is the family social network map, which traces family and nonfamily communications, behaviors, emotional ties, social status, functions, and other connections. In substance abuse treatment, a social network assessment allows counselors to identify significant parties with key roles in a client's substance abuse trajectory. Because the concept of family has significantly expanded in modern times to include nonrelatives of considerable importance (a boyfriend or girlfriend or same-sex partner, friends, religious leaders, formal and informal social groups, etc.), social network mapping and analysis can be of considerable additional importance.

78. D: The Community Oriented Program Environment Scale (CPES) measures the actual, preferred, and expected treatment environment or programmatic social climate. These perceptions are measured over time and designed to improve communication and treatment efficacy. The CPES dimensional components include staff involvement, support, spontaneity, autonomy, practical orientation, personal problems orientation, program clarity, staff control, and anger and aggression.

79. C: APs demonstrate their scope of practice through specialized education and training on the science of addiction, supervised experience in addiction, and skills required to deliver addiction-specific services. Scope of practice is designed to protect clients from inadequate, fraudulent, ineffective, unethical, or illegal practices. Standards of practice refer to activities that are evidence-based practices for mental disorders and SUDs.

80. B: The term *authentically connected referral network* refers to a carefully established set of service providers prepared to meet client needs as they evolve. Key elements to the network are: (1) established communication linkages to facilitate timely sharing of information with client consent; (2) a focus on community-wide outcomes, ensuring that best interests are being met and that community education ensures understandings about substance abuse; (3) a primary focus on meeting client needs through collaboration as opposed to exclusionary rules; (4) consistency and credibility in conduct to ensure both interagency and client confidence and trust. The goal is for all network agencies and providers to recognize their valued and essential roles in the addiction treatment process and for clients to recognize this and respond with similar trust and confidence. Lastly, treatment is designed to be conducted concurrently rather than post-discharge.

81. B: The behavioral group model is grounded in the assumption that substance use originates from behaviors that are learned and reinforced over time. Behavioral modification is accomplished through a variety of interventions such as: (1) identifying the conditioned stimuli that trigger specific addictive behaviors; (2) producing ways to avoid conditioned stimuli; (3) creating contingency management strategies (relapse prevention strategies); and (4) desensitizing stimuli-response patterns. The cognitive-behavioral approach recognizes that addiction results from the dynamic interplay of multiple variables. Cognitive-behavioral therapy groups change perceptions, beliefs, and thinking patterns to alter relapse behaviors and reinforce positive social networks to offer support for change.

82. D: Client assessment, evaluations, and need for referrals occurs on an ongoing basis, while planning for aftercare to begin at the point of intial client contact. Information gleaned on an ongoing basis also relevant in the aftercare planning process. Family members should be drawn into aftercare planning and education early on to ensure ongoing understanding and support.

83. A: Education, vocational training, and employment issues are core support concerns but do not constitute adjunctive therapies. Adjunctive therapies are used to enhance the emotional and psychological functioning and include but are not limited to stress management, medication, and acupuncture. Mediation techniques include approaches such as mindfulness (learning to appreciate the present), visualization (positive imagery), breath meditation (learning to focus and control thinking and the body), and transcendental meditation (deep awareness and consciousness). As an adjunct to substance abuse treatment, meditation is in harmony with the intent and philosophy of twelve-step and other mutual self-help groups.

84. D: Amphetamine is a synthetic substance. Caffeine, nicotine, and cocaine are all naturally existing substances.

85. A: Much like all cultural identities, the cultural identities of American Indians and Alaska Natives are constantly in flux and historically formed. Although there are individual differences among these cultures, many have beliefs and values grounded in respect for their elders and are influenced by generational stories (e.g., oral tradition). Identities are historically formed and are shaped by the present-day repercussions of colonization and the associated historical trauma. Cultural identities are constantly in flux in response to various experiences, acculturation, evolving statuses, role shifts, and social determinants.

86. B: Attributes of cultural humility include openness, authenticity, and self-awareness. Principle III-21 of the NAADAC Code of Ethics (2021) states that APs must deliver culturally responsive counseling, encompassing multicultural knowledge, cultural humility, and an openness to cultural differences. Cultural humility is attained through intentional focus; reflection; and awareness of one's own cultural biases, values, and assumptions. It is an other-oriented, lifelong process where APs remain teachable (rather than as the "expert") and self-critical to address power imbalances and inequities in the provider–client dyad.

87. C: Karen uses broaching to engage Amy in intentional discussions concerning cross-cultural experiences and the similarities and differences in their cultures. Broaching is associated with cultural humility with dialogue that is open, purposeful, respectful, and authentic. Breaking occurs when individuals take a one-sided and uninformed outlook on cultural differences, causing them to reject any knowledge or understanding of differing cultures. Bridging, which is the opposite of breaking, occurs when individuals turn outside themselves to seek a means to build common ground. Bridging differs from broaching in that broaching is used in the context of cultural humility. Cultural brokering is the process of using an intermediary to bridge cultural divisions between differing groups, persons, or systems.

88. A: Motivational enhancement therapy (MET) is an adaptation of motivational interviewing (MI). MET uses MI strategies and techniques but also incorporates structured assessments and follow-up sessions. In these sessions, clients are provided feedback regarding substance use in multiple areas (e.g., societal norms and their level of use, physical and social consequences, relevant family history, readiness for change, and associated risk factors). This normative feedback is reviewed in a nonconfrontational manner by means of MI techniques (client-centered counseling to explore and resolve treatment ambivalence and achieve lasting changes). In this way, MET informs while also eliciting motivation to change by resolving ambivalence, evoking self-motivational statements, revealing a commitment to change, and rolling with resistance (e.g., responding neutrally to resistance rather than contradicting or correcting). MET is effective with all degrees of substance abuse, and court-mandated clients appear to benefit as much as self-referred clients. A four-session version of MET was found to be as effective as the other, more intensive interventions (i.e., cognitive-behavioral therapy [CBT] and twelve-step facilitation). Clients with anger issues achieved significantly more abstinent days.

89. C: Oppression refers to the unfair and unjust use of social power to deprive subgroups of the resources needed to lead safe, productive, and fulfilling lives. Oppression is protected, justified, and maintained by sociocultural norms and laws that create inequities that drive behavioral health disparities. Examples of oppression include ageism, classism, heterosexism, racism, and anti-Semitism. Prejudice is a biased thought or attitude against certain groups. Racism is a form of prejudice that operates on stereotypes and assumptions that one race is superior to another. Microaggressions are brief, commonplace slights or indignities that communicate hostility, derogatory insults, or negative behaviors toward another group.

90. D: Caleb's relationship with his mother is not indicative of structural racism but is likely reflective of a traditional (i.e., patriarchal) cultural expectation. Structural racism is embedded in institutions and social structures and has the potential to negatively affect treatment for substance use disorder (SUD) and co-occurring mental disorders. Structural racism is evident in Caleb's psychiatric diagnoses, his father's prison sentence, and his discharge summary (i.e., noncompliance with psychotropic medication). Black males are disproportionately diagnosed with schizophrenia and are more likely to be labeled as aggressive, resistant, angry, and noncompliant. Stiffer penalties and harsher sentencing for black males that intensified during the war on drugs in the 1980s persist. Caleb's discharge summary reflects the larger trend of racial disparities in prescribing antipsychotics.

91. C: Although the American Society of Addiction Medicine (ASAM) seeks to place clients in the least restrictive setting, ASAM does not use a client's diagnosis to determine appropriate levels of care. Instead, ASAM incorporates several domains and principles, including but not limited to matching the client's level of safety with the appropriate intensity of services, individualizing and integrating treatment for addiction and co-occurring disorders, and incorporating the client's right to direct treatment on an ongoing basis.

92. C: Because Caleb engages in unprotected sex with other men, postexposure prophylaxis would be the most beneficial harm reduction strategy. Harm reduction strategies help reduce morbidity (i.e., disease) and mortality rates among at-risk individuals. Caleb is at risk for human immunodeficiency virus (HIV), viral hepatitis, and sexually transmitted infections, making postexposure prophylaxis an appropriate strategy. A needle exchange program is less beneficial for Caleb because he reports smoking methamphetamine. Methadone is a treatment for opioid use disorder, with some research suggesting that methadone increases concurrent stimulant use. A safety plan is not a common harm reduction strategy.

93. B: There are currently no FDA-approved medications for stimulant use disorder. Evidence-based practices include contingency management, cognitive-behavioral therapy, and the use of screening, brief intervention, and motivational interviewing.

94. A: The Child and Adolescent Level of Care/Service Intensity Utilization System is used to determine the intensity of treatment services for children and adolescents, with lower scores assisting with early recognition of treatment issues requiring basic or low-intensity services. This assessment tool is limited in that it cannot prescribe a specific treatment plan or placement environment and cannot provide a clinical diagnosis. Because of these limitations, the instrument should not be used without the contribution of clinical knowledge, judgment, and expertise.

95. D: A study reported significantly less cocaine use by the Matrix patients at eight months after treatment admission (monthly or more frequent cocaine use was four of thirty in the Matrix group, as compared to ten of twenty-three following inpatient treatment, and fourteen of thirty receiving no formal treatment). Another study revealed dramatic methamphetamine use reductions during treatment (eleven days of use in the past thirty at enrollment, reduced to about four days at treatment's end, decreasing to three days at twelve-month follow-up). A study of one hundred cocaine-dependent subjects randomly assigned to a six-month Matrix treatment condition versus other available community resources revealed fewer positive urine tests for Matrix subjects but not for community resource subjects at three and six-month follow-ups. Similarly, improved scores on the Addiction Severity Index (ASI) employment and family scales, and on a depression scale, were noted. Finally, in an eight-site study coordinated by the University of California, Los Angeles (UCLA), the program completion rate for Matrix participants was significantly higher (40.9 percent) than for treatment-as-usual participants (34.2 percent).

96. C: Guidelines for managing access to a client's electronic health record include using two-factor authentication, having a secure password, and limiting individual access on a need-to-know basis. Media sanitation permanently destroys data and includes irreversible processes such as clearing or overwriting, purging (e.g., block erasing), and destroying (e.g., incinerating).

97. B: Only mandated reporting information, such as child abuse, can be disclosed without a client's written consent. This includes any information about whether a client is receiving treatment or what he or she may be receiving treatment for, even to an employer paying for the treatment. Further, non-court-ordered information cannot be released even to a law enforcement agency or to any other interested party without the client's written consent. A properly informed client is one who is aware of: (1) to whom or what entity the information is being released; (2) the full purpose for the release; (3) the specific information to be released; and (4) when the information release expires. Client confidentiality regarding substance abuse treatment is protected by 42 CFR Part 2 and HIPAA.

98. D: Homework assignments associated with short-term goal attainment are typically not included on a client's treatment plan. The key components of a treatment plan include: (1) problem statements, which are based on information obtained during the assessment; (2) goal statements, which are derived from the problem statements; (3) objectives, which consist of what the client will do to meet treatment goals; and (4) interventions, which are defined as what the staff will do to assist the client. Relevant client strengths are often a required component. It is often useful to draw problems from a master problem list. The list should include all identified problems, regardless of available program services, and whether they should be immediately addressed or deferred. Identification of problems is a shared client-counselor endeavor. Problem statements should be nonjudgmental, jargon-free, and written in complete sentences. Couch problem statements in behavioral specifics to ease writing goals, objectives, and interventions.

99. B: An example of the psychological effects of a psychoactive substance is delusional thinking. Physical effects of substance use include lethargy, itching, and dizziness. Delusions are mental or psychological, as opposed to physical effects, which are physiological in nature. Physical effects of drug use are more strongly associated with tolerance, withdrawal, dependence, and toxicity.

100. C: A client's motivation for change is internal, whereas clients who enter treatment as the result of family pressure or a court order may not be motivated to change their behavior. Motivation for behavioral change is a personal and internal matter, with a greater likelihood of ultimate success. Assessing motivation may be pursued via the Stages of Change Readiness and Treatment Eagerness Scale (SOCRATES). It is a nineteen-item self-report instrument comprised of three main scales—recognition, ambivalence, and taking Steps—requiring approximately three minutes to complete. Those in the pre-contemplation stage typically deny the problem. Clients in the preparation and action stages typically admit that they have a problem. Optimal treatment planning requires an understanding of where a client is in the change readiness process, which also promotes more effective exploration of the current barriers to further change.

101. D: Emotional distress is a withdrawal symptom that is common among most substances recognized in the DSM-5-TR. Substance-related and addictive disorders change the brain's reward circuitry and reinforce repeated use. Withdrawal symptoms, including depression and anxiety, result from dysregulated brain reward systems. Fatigue frequently occurs during withdrawal from stimulants. Psychomotor agitation, nausea, and vomiting are commonly experienced during withdrawal from CNS depressants (e.g., sedatives).

102. B: Research consistently reveals that the therapeutic alliance is of primary importance in clients achieving positive outcome. Among the many positive effects of the therapeutic alliance, treatment retention is one of the most significant. Consequently, achieving and maintaining a therapeutic alliance is crucial. The four key components of an effective therapeutic alliance are: (1) the client's capacity to purposefully work on the problem (providing a shared goal and common ground); (2) the affective (emotional) bond between the client and the therapist; (3) the therapist's possession of an empathic understanding of the client; and (4) agreement on the primary goals and between client and therapist. Counselors can enhance the therapeutic alliance by being empathic, nonjudgmental, and active listeners and by actively presenting the treatment process as a collaborative venture, rather than as one consisting of unilateral directives.

103. B: According to Principle III-21 of the NAADAC/ NCC AP Code of Ethics (2021), Addition professionals (APs) provide referrals for clients to address a client's holistic needs fully. In doing so, APs seek culturally and linguistically appropriate resources when an impairment is beyond an AP's scope of practice. The scope of practice includes educational competencies, knowledge, certification, training, skills, or licensure. While resources must also be developmentally appropriate, it would be rare for resources to be educationally appropriate for the client. Similarly, it would be increasingly rare for resources to be financially or administratively appropriate.

104. A: Community reinforcement (CRT) and contingency management (CM) are most effective when paired together. CRT uses psychoeducation to decrease stigma and teach families that substance use is a disease rather than a moral failing. This method also encourages family members to engage in activities to lead purposeful lives, regardless of how the individual family member's recovery is progressing. Contingency management involves positive reinforcement (e.g., gift cards, tokens, privileges) for individuals in recovery who maintain their sobriety and engage in targeted behaviors (e.g., negative urine screens). Because a return to baseline substance use can follow the termination of CM, in particular, more long-term supports (such as twelve-step program involvement) may be needed for more enduring success. Maximum benefits accrue with larger rewards that increase in value to maintain CM motivation. By contrast, CRT typically involves rewards from more-enduring sources (e.g., family, job, pleasurable activities) that can more naturally persist after treatment completion. Even so, education in relationship enhancement, goal setting and attainment, balanced lifestyle, and so on can more fully ensure long-term treatment benefits. Finally, rewards and other reinforcements must be consistently applied and only provided in response to measurable successes (e.g., extended negative-result urine screens).

105. B: Treatment plan goals, tasks, and objectives are most effective when designed by the client and counselor. The client and counselor determine the focus of treatment and carefully negotiate client-driven and counselor-directed goals. Components of a treatment plan include mutually agreed-upon problems, measurable short-term and long-term goals and objectives, treatment modes (e.g., individual, group, family), task assignments, and theoretical techniques and interventions. Carefully constructed treatment plans are individualized and include biological, psychological, social, and cultural elements specific to the client. The therapist should only decide on components of the treatment plan with the client's active agreement. Both the client and therapist may be told by the therapist's clinic what they will be doing together in therapy. While many clinics adhere to specific treatment philosophies and methods, the therapist and client should still collaborate in mutually agreeable ways within those parameters.

106. A: Probing is a direct request or question designed to stimulate discussion or arrive at a particular conclusion. In a screening, probing helps to accurately evaluate risk, provide praise and affirm positive choices, and/or educate on the dangers of alcohol use. Summarizing is used to bring together certain concepts and themes. Clarification is used when counselors seek to understand a client's unclear thoughts, emotions, or behaviors. Confirmation is not regarded as a counseling technique.

107. A: Evidence-based treatment for pregnant people with OUD includes the recommendation for buprenorphine and methadone treatment, which is safe for the mother and fetus. Medication for OUD is a harm reduction measure used to prevent overdose and other health problems for the mother and developing fetus. Medically supervised withdrawal is neither safe nor advisable due to the risks of overdose and fetal distress symptoms (e.g., high blood pressure, tachycardia). Breastfeeding while taking methadone or buprenorphine is safe, suggested, and beneficial. Pregnant people who switch from buprenorphine to methadone can do so safely; however, switching from methadone to buprenorphine or from buprenorphine to naltrexone during pregnancy is not recommended due to the risk of withdrawal symptoms.

108. B: The study of pharmacokinetics includes the processes of absorption, distribution, metabolism, and excretion properties (i.e., ADME). Pharmacokinetics is the study of how the human body interacts with substances from when the substance is ingested to the moment the substance leaves the body. Absorption occurs when the unmetabolized drug moves into a person's bloodstream and is dependent on the substance's route of administration (e.g., inhalation, orally, the drug's formulation and properties, and how the drug interacts with food in the GI system. Metabolism refers to how the substance is broken down, while excretion refers to the method by which the substance is removed from the body. Finally, distribution determines the disbursement of a substance as it moves through the body's bloodstream and tissues, contributing to the substance's efficacy and toxicity.

109. D: The Code of Federal Regulations requires that information, even about the mere presence of a client in treatment, is not to be released under any circumstances unless a qualified court hearing has first been held wherein the issue of confidentiality and client needs have first been addressed. Following this, a special authorizing order must be issued per 42 CFR § 2.65b. At a hearing, the court must determine: (1) if the alleged crime is sufficiently serious (e.g., homicide, rape, assault with a deadly weapon) to warrant breaching confidentiality in this sensitive area; (2) if the records disclosure will be of sufficient value in the investigation; (3) if other reasonably effective options exist; (4) if the potential for damage to the client, to the client-provider relationship, and to the program's ability to continue providing services outweighs the release of this very sensitive information; and (5) if the applicant is acting in a true law enforcement function and if adequate counsel has been obtained by the records holder or agency.

110. C: Bruce Tuckman's group model includes five phases: forming, storming, norming, performing, and adjourning. Forming involves engagement, exchanging information, and creating bonds. The key characteristics are tentative overtures, polite exchanges, and worries about fitting in. Storming involves dissatisfaction, disagreement, competition, and conflict. Key characteristics are criticizing ideas, interrupting, hostility, power struggles, and forming factions. Norming involves forming group structure, establishing roles and relationships, developing cohesion, and creating harmony. Key characteristics are seeking consensus, reaching agreements, building support, and achieving a sense of "we" in endeavors. Performing involves task focus, productivity, and identifying achievements. Key characteristics are cooperation, problem-solving, and decision-making. Finally, adjourning consists of completing tasks, ending duties, and preparing for termination. Key characteristics are managing emotions (e.g., sadness, anxiety) surrounding termination, a sense of accomplishment, and disbanding.

111. D: The question "How many times in your life have you been charged with driving while intoxicated?" can be found on the Addiction Severity Index, which assesses addiction severity in seven areas: medical, work, drug use, alcohol use, legal difficulties, family/social status, and psychiatric status. The Patient Health Questionnaire asks about appetite and overeating, whereas the Alcohol Use Disorders Identification Test is a 10-item questionnaire that asks about blackouts and flashbacks. Lastly, the Drug Abuse Screening Test-10 asks about being charged with driving while intoxicated.

112. B: The therapist must first determine if the grandmother has legal guardianship. The client is court-ordered to attend therapy in lieu of criminal charges. Client autonomy must be respected, but the family therapist would provide therapy regardless of the client's desire to change or whether the grandmother chooses to be an active participant. Although a handful of states allow minors as young as 12 to consent to mental health or substance abuse treatment, the client lacks the capacity to provide voluntary informed consent after being diagnosed with intellectual developmental disorder. We know that the mother is in prison, but her parental rights could still be intact, and we do not know about the father's whereabouts and rights. Proof of guardianship should be provided at the outset of therapy. Many grandparents in similar circumstances have informal agreements and cannot provide consent for treatment.

113. B: The addiction process involves the following cycles: binge/intoxication, withdrawal/negative affect, and preoccupation/anticipation. The cyclical patterns of addiction reinforce the notion that addiction is a chronic brain disease with the potential for recurrence and recovery.

114. D: Tre's drinking and drug use are positively reinforced by peer approval. Behaviors that encompass the addiction cycle include positive reinforcement, negative reinforcement, impulsivity, and compulsivity. Positive reinforcement involves pairing a stimulus (e.g., drug use) with a reinforcing response (e.g., pleasure, peer approval). Negative reinforcement occurs when substances provide relief or take away something unpleasant (e.g., avoiding withdrawal symptoms). Impulsivity is the inability to resist an urge or to engage in behavior without considering the consequences. Compulsivity occurs when an individual continues repetitive substance use in the face of adverse outcomes.

115. D: In adherence to Principle II-9 of the NAADAC Code of Ethics (2021), the therapist should respond to the court's request by limiting the disclosure as narrowly as possible to prevent client harm. Court reports include general information, such as dates of services, compliance with requests (e.g., drug screens), attendance, progress toward treatment plan goals, and any relevant treatment recommendations. The client does not have the intellectual capacity to assent to services. Principle I-31 of the code disallows APs withholding records needed for treatment solely based on nonpayment. Court letters are part of a client's record. Supplying the court with a treatment summary would require a signed release of information rather than a subpoena.

116. B: According to Principle I-21 of the NAADAC Code of Ethics, the AP should first provide the client with a culturally-appropriate referral. Principle I-21 states that APs strive to meet each client's biopsychosocial and spiritual needs. APs must refer to culturally appropriate resources when a client presents any impairment beyond the AP's scope of practice. Because the client is a conservative Muslim female with the sole diagnosis of alcohol use disorder (i.e., no co-occurring mental disorder), it is likely that religious prohibition of alcohol, minority stress, stigma, and gender norms, contribute to the marital difficulties. The AP must seek consultation and connect the client with online or in-person resources and supports if there are no culturally-appropriate referral sources available. While seeking education and training in cultural diversity is helpful, it does not sufficiently target the client's immediate need as the counselor would not be able to apply this training with the client right away. Inviting a "qualified therapist" to participate is vague and impractical.

117. D: The integrated treatment for co-occurring disorders refers to all-inclusive treatment for mental health and substance use disorders. Clinicians use biopsychosocial-spiritual assessments to detect the presence of co-occurring disorders and create individualized treatment plans. Integrated care involves treating both conditions simultaneously, while sequential treatment involves treating each condition separately and parallel treatment involves participation in two separate treatment regimens.

118. D: Women tend to initiate substance use in relation to a partner, spouse, or family member's use and in the presence of a co-occurring mood or eating disorder. Clinical assessments must also consider the effects of trauma and abuse, which is higher in women diagnosed with substance use disorder (SUD) than in women without SUD. Transgender women diagnosed with SUD experience even greater incidences of sexual violence. Further, gender-related differences are age-dependent, with females between the ages of 12 and 17 being more likely than men to have higher rates of SUD. Women tend to resist treatment due to stigma, particularly when pregnant or parenting, due to perceived threats of social or legal consequences. Experts advocate for person-centered, trauma-informed therapy delivered in a safe and nurturing environment.

119. C: Individuals whose cocaine use is considered isolated do not go on to develop cocaine use disorder. Cocaine use disorder begins with experimental use, which is motivated by curiosity and characterized by non-punitive consequences. The second stage is frequent or social use. In this phase, individuals tend to use cocaine socially or turn to the substance when in emotional pain. In the third stage, individuals are less likely to have control over the amount used. Finally, dysfunctional use is characterized by preoccupation with drug use, chronic sleep and health problems, severe disruptions in social and family life, and work and financial issues. In the final phase, the person becomes dependent on cocaine and generally cannot stop without assistance.

120. B: This theory posits that present and future behavior arises from the consequences (positive or negative) of past behavior. Substances used can provide both positively reinforcing effects (euphoria, etc.) and negative reinforcement (relief of psychic pain, avoidance of withdrawal, etc.). Desire for abstinence is typically an insufficient motivation, particularly at the outset. Therefore, other rewards that reinforce abstinence and a positive lifestyle change are usually required. Both community reinforcement (CR) and contingency management (CM) approaches motivate behavioral change and support abstinence by consistently rewarding desirable behaviors and ignoring or punishing other negative behaviors. CR uses relationships and other important life aspects—family and friends, job, hobbies, social events— to produce positive reinforcement. CM uses tangible rewards (events or objects) and punishments (fines, losses of privileges, etc.) to extinguish desires for substance abuse. Quitting one substance first may be a better goal than attempting to abstain from all substances. Starting with small changes can be a very effective strategy. Further, more frequent reinforcers (even if small), may be more effective than larger, more-distant rewards or punishments.

121. A: Bowen family systems theory views the family as an integrated emotional unit, best described and understood via a systems perspective when attempting to describe the complex interactions that arise in the unit. Family members are intensely emotionally connected and profoundly influence the feelings, thoughts, and actions of each other. They seek attention, support, and approval from each other and respond to one another's distress, needs, and expectations. Changes in the functioning of any one member will be followed by reciprocal changes in the others. From this perspective, family genograms, disruption history (e.g., immigration, holocaust), individual questioning, and orienting the members toward facts (versus reactions) can help improve family understandings and function. Coaching individuals into changes in interaction patterns can reduce triangulation and overall family anxiety.

122. C: The CAGE questionnaire quickly screens for alcohol abuse by asking for a "yes" or "no" response to four questions: (1) Have you ever felt the need to cut down on your drinking; (2) do you feel annoyed by people complaining about your drinking; (3) do you ever feel guilty about your drinking; and (4) do you ever drink an eye-opener in the morning to relieve the shakes? Two or more "yes" responses are clinically significant; however, it is recommended that primary care physicians identify scores of one or more to appropriately serve all individuals who may have an alcohol use disorder.

123. C: The ASAM multidimensional assessment includes six dimensions, with dimension 2, "Biomedical conditions and complications," measuring the client's ability to tolerate and cope with physical discomfort. Dimension 2 assesses the severity of medical issues and determines if the client's biomedical problems are chronic or acute and which symptoms may interfere with recovery. Dimension 6, "Recovering/Living environment," determines if the client's current living situation has the potential to endanger or support their recovery. Dimension 3, "Emotional, behavioral, or cognitive conditions and complications," explores whether there are co-occurring disorders that, if confirmed, would impair the client's capacity to function independently. Lastly, dimension 1, "Acute intoxication and/or withdrawal potential," assesses a client's withdrawal history, any sudden discontinuation of a substance, and any current symptoms of withdrawal.

124. C: The Substance Abuse and Mental Health Services Administration (SAMHSA) maintains the National Registry of Evidence-Based Programs and Practices (NREPP), which is a database of evidence-supported approaches to substance abuse counseling. The goal is to make available those theories, strategies, programs, and practices that have been proven effective in the treatment of substance abuse disorders. The database includes approaches such as twelve-step facilitation therapy, cognitive-behavioral therapy (CBT), and motivational interviewing (MI), among others.

The database offers evaluations, recommendations, and suggestions to optimize the effectiveness of the various programs reviewed. The database is readily accessible via the Internet, and counselors should become familiar with the various programs, techniques, theories, and approaches offered to ensure optimal practices and program outcome effectiveness.

125. D: The Symptom Checklist-90-R (SCL-90-R) is normed on individuals aged 13 and older. The SCL-90-R is used to assess a broad range of psychological problems and key symptoms of psychopathology. The instrument is also used to measure client progress or treatment outcomes. Containing only ninety items and a five-point rating scale, the SCL-90-R can be completed in as little as twelve to fifteen minutes. The SCL-90-R produces an overview of distressing symptoms for the "past week" (e.g., "For the past week, how much were you bothered by headaches?"). The nine primary symptom dimensions measured are: somatization, obsessive-compulsive, interpersonal sensitivity, depression, anxiety, hostility, phobic anxiety, paranoid ideation, and psychoticism. The index of symptom severity facilitates treatment decisions and identifies problems before they become acute.

126. C: The first thing the counselor should before reviewing a client's assessment results is to acknowledge the client's efforts in responding to the tests and provide positive reinforcement by stating your appreciation. This aids rapport and facilitates the client's ensuing positive responses. After this, you should ask if the client experienced any difficulties with testing. Additional steps include asking the client if there were any problems with the assessment, whether the assessment evoked any changed perceptions about their substance use, and if there are any additional questions. Following the client's responses, it is important to indicate that your correct interpretation of test findings may require the client's assistance, and encourage the client to ask any questions along the way.

127. D: Data, Assessment, and Plan notes help clinicians organize documentation, select appropriate goals, and track client progress. In the data section, clinicians record salient facts, including but not limited to client statements, mood and behavioral observations, mental status, response to intervention, and any available quantifiable measures. This section is typically the longest portion of a DAP note. The assessment section includes the clinician's interpretation of the session and incorporates a tentative or working diagnosis, suicidality (when applicable), and a review of the client's treatment plan. It may also include the client's motivation or ability to proceed. The plan section includes session scheduling and the expected focus for upcoming treatment sessions. In this area, the clinician provides the client with homework involving actionable steps and, when applicable, referrals to outside sources.

128. D: Recreational therapy was not one of the core features and services referenced by the Center for Substance Abuse Treatment (CSAT). The CAST consensus panel agreed that intensive outpatient treatment (IOT) core features and services must include the following: intake and orientation; full biopsychosocial assessment; individualized treatment planning; individual, family, and group counseling; psychoeducational programming; case management; linkages with mutual-help and community-based support groups; twenty-four-hour crisis support; medical treatment; formal drug screening and monitoring (urine or breath tests); educational and vocational services; psychiatric evaluation and psychotherapy; medication management; and discharge planning and transition (discharge) services. They further defined potential enhanced services to include: adult education; recreational activities; housing and food resources, smoking cessation treatment; transportation referrals; child care; and parenting skills education.

129. D: Goals for clinical supervision include protecting clients' well-being, promoting professional and ethical practices, and empowering the supervisee to grow in their ability to self-supervise. The supervisor is also used to monitor the supervisee's job performance. Clinical supervisors do not function as counselors for supervisees. Supervisees who present with personal or professional difficulties that require counseling are encouraged to seek their own therapists.

130. B: Metabolism alters the composition of the drug. Metabolism is a process by which an ingested drug is changed into a form that can be removed from the body. The faster the drug moves through a person's system, the sooner the effects of the drug are diminished.

131. B: The American Society of Addiction Medicine (ASAM) recognizes four levels of treatment placement and five specific levels of care. The lowest level (referred to as Level 0.5) is designated as early intervention, which refers to education and other services for individuals with at-risk behaviors but for whom a substance abuse diagnosis cannot be confirmed. Level I consists of basic nonresidential outpatient services, primarily education, counseling, and behavioral change. Level II offers Intensive outpatient or partial hospitalization (inpatient evenings or weekends, etc.). The focus is on comprehensive biopsychosocial assessments and individualized treatment plans. Level III consists of residential or inpatient treatment and offers a planned regimen of care in a twenty-four-hour live-in setting. Level IV is medically managed intensive inpatient treatment. Level IV provides twenty-four-hour medically directed evaluation and treatment of substance-related and mental disorders in an acute care setting.

132. C: Roberts' seven-stage crisis intervention model includes (1) conducting a crisis and biopsychosocial assessment, (2) establishing rapport, (3) identifying aspects of the crisis or presenting problem, (4) exploring underlying emotions, (5) generating alternative responses, (6) formulating a plan of action, and (7) creating a follow-up plan.

133. A: In the DSM-5-TR, the term "racialized" is used instead of "race/racial." The DSM-5-TR uses the term "ethnoracial" to reflect US Census Bureau categories that combine race and ethnicity (e.g., African-American, Hispanic, or white people). The term "minority" is not used because it reinforces social hierarchies.

134. B: Successful behavioral crisis response systems for suicide, substance use, and mental health involve implementing a crisis response continuum of care, to include outreach and engagement, crisis call centers, mobile crisis teams, crisis stabilization, and postcrisis support. A successful crisis response increases reliance on trained behavioral health providers and seeks to eliminate the overinvolvement of law enforcement and the criminal justice system. Providing monetary incentives for medication for OUD is a harm reduction strategy rather than a crisis response.

135. B: The DSM-5-TR does not include withdrawal symptoms for hallucinogens and inhalants due to the lack of empirical evidence to substantiate clinically significant symptoms. The DSM-5-TR applies the diagnosis of SUD for the following substances: alcohol, caffeine, cannabis, hallucinogens, phencyclidine, other hallucinogens, inhalants, opioids, sedatives, stimulants, tobacco, and other unknown substances.

136. B: Nephrosis is a kidney disorder and is not induced by alcohol. Alcohol is metabolized by the liver, which makes it particularly susceptible to its toxic effects Steatosis consists of fatty deposits in the liver that, if severe, can prove fatal. Alcoholic hepatitis is characterized by abdominal pain, nausea, vomiting, and an inflamed liver. In more extreme cases, jaundice and bleeding can result. Jaundice (a yellowing of the skin and whites of the eyes) is from bilirubin, a by-product of aging red blood cells broken down in the liver, that should have been fully metabolized by the liver. Spontaneous bleeding occurs because key clotting factors are made in the liver, but production is inhibited by hepatitis. Cirrhosis refers to scarring of the liver from alcohol damage, preventing its normal functioning. High blood toxins can also cause hepatic encephalopathy—a reversible dementia—if the toxins are reduced.

137. D: Burnout among counselors and APs involves depersonalization, reduced professional efficacy, and emotional exhaustion. Depersonalization is the process of detaching from clients and often involves cynicism or an inability to show empathy or compassion. Burnout involves feeling as if one lacks professional accomplishments. Emotional exhaustion results from an inability to meet multiple demands. Vicarious trauma is similar to burnout but is caused by repeated exposure to trauma.

138. D: This approach was developed to assist those with persistent mental illness to transition from institutional care to independent living. Two foundational principles are: (1) assisting clients in assuming direct control over their own search for resources (e.g., transportation, housing, employment, etc.), and (2) drawing upon clients' strengths in the acquisition of resources. This model focuses on informal helping networks (rather than institutional networks), supported through the client-case manager relationship. To achieve goals, the case manager maintains an active client outreach. The strengths case management perspective is used with substance abusers for three reasons: (1) case management facilitates client responsibility in finding and accessing resources needed for an enduring recovery; (2) the advocacy component counters the belief that substance abusers are morally deficient or in denial and thus unworthy of support; and (3) the emphasis on client strengths, assets, and abilities counterbalances treatment models that emphasize pathology and disease. Advocacy and client-driven goal planning can at times cause stress between the case manager and other members of a treatment team, but the approach clearly leads to improved client outcomes.

139. C: The Code of Federal Regulations (CFR) Part 2 protects the confidentiality of substance abuse patient records without patient consent. The SAMHSA US Department of Health and Human Service Confidentiality of Substance Use Disorder Patient Records (Revised 2020), 42 CFR Part 2 protects patient records of those treated, being treated, or seeking treatment for substance use disorder (SUD) in federally funded programs. Part 2 is designed to reduce stigma and encourage treatment participation by providing enhanced confidentiality for individuals with SUD. It differs from HIPAA protections in that Part 2 only applies to SUD treatment, whereas HIPAA applies to general health information. Part 2 prohibits disclosures for treatment and payment unless the patient provides consent. Part 2 does not permit disclosures without consent unless a legitimate medical emergency exists. Lastly, a court order is required to disclose records to be used in criminal investigations.

140. B: The abstinence violation effect occurs when people blame factors beyond their control for relapsing. It is used when individuals believe that there is no intermediary response to relapse—that they cannot remain abstinent due to external factors or factors beyond control (e.g., lack of willpower, relationships). Seemingly irrelevant decisions are a cognitive response to relapse involving the tendency to overlook more minor causes by focusing on larger areas of concern. The problem of immediate gratification is the tendency to use substances to satisfy urges and cravings while ignoring the long-term consequences. Covert antecedents occur when clients attribute the cause of their relapse to unanticipated events (e.g., stress level, interpersonal difficulties).

141. A: Counselor use attending by adopting s a relaxed body posture, maintaining eye contact, and speaks in an even, pleasant tone. Empathizing is the ability of a counselor to place themselves in their client's shoes. Genuineness describes a counselor's displays of authenticity, congruence between words and actions, and a shared connection between the client and counselor. Counselors use concreteness to reduce ambiguity, provide focus, and keep the conversation on track.

142. A: Stewardship refers to the judicious and conscientious use of available resource. Justice refers to the fair, just, and equal treatment of others. Candor describes truth in dealing with clients, associates, and coworkers. Obedience involves adherence to legal and ethical directives.

143. B: Psychomotor agitation is a common withdrawal symptom for alcohol, stimulants, and sedative/tranquilizers. Withdrawal symptoms from cannabis include insomnia, irritability, weight changes, anxiety, and depression.

144. C: Once the NAADAC Ethics Committee determines that a complaint or grievance is valid, recommendations may include requests to attend an ethics workshop or class. The committee cannot refund money owed to anyone due to violations of billing or financial procedures because that is a civil matter. The committee does not have the authority to terminate a member's state licensure or certification, nor does it have the authority to suspend anyone from providing clinical services.

145. B: CRAFFT is designed specifically for use with adolescents, drawing upon situations that are common to this age group. The instrument derives its name from the key word in each of the screening questions: driving a car while intoxicated; using alcohol or drugs to relax, feel better, or fit in; using alcohol or drug when alone; forgetting events that occurred while using alcohol or drugs; requests by family or friends to limit use; and, getting into trouble while using alcohol or drugs. The other instruments are: AUDIT (Alcohol Use Disorders Identification Test); the CAGE (also an acronym: needing to cut down drinking, feeling annoyed at drinking criticism, feeling guilty at drinking, and needing a morning eye-opener drink); and, the MAST (Michigan Alcoholism Screening Test).

146. C: Compared to men, women tend to use substances for a larger variety of reasons (e.g., to treat chronic pain or to cope with mental disorders). There are several sex and gender differences in substance use. Compared to men, women who use certain substances are more likely to be diagnosed with depression or anxiety. Women also tend to use smaller amounts of some substances for a shorter duration before developing SUD. Lastly, men are more likely to use nearly all types of illicit substances.

147. C: Drugs most often leave the body after metabolization through a person's urine. Depending upon the level of efficiency, the liver and kidneys work together to break the drug down and excrete it out of the body in the form of urine. Other forms of excretion include sweat, tears, breastmilk, feces, and reproductive fluids (e.g., semen).

148. A: The Texas Christian University (TCU) Drug Screen 5 determines the severity of substance use and the appropriate level of care. TCU Drug Screen 5 is frequently used in criminal justice settings and can be administered to adults and adolescents. However, it is also appropriate for use in the general population. TCU Drug Screen 5 is a 17-item instrument with criteria for tolerance, withdrawal, and frequency of use. A Likert scale is used to determine the severity of the substance use from mild, moderate, and severe and can help determine a client's appropriate level of care. The TCU Drug Screen 5 can be used in an interview setting, or it can be self-administered.

149. B: Guiding principles of treatment planning are represented by the acronym MARTS. The first treatment planning principles: M = measurable. Goals and objectives must be clearly measurable so that progress and other changes can be identified readily and documented. A = attainable. Goals and objectives, and interventions as well, must be achievable (attainable) during the active treatment phase. T = time limited. The active focus of treatment should be on short-term or time-limited goals and objectives. R = realistic. It must be realistic for a client to complete the identified objectives of each goal within the specified time period. S = specific. Objectives, and associated interventions, must be sufficiently specific and goal focused to ensure progress toward attainment. A key element is involving the client directly in the planning process to ensure that the goals, objectives, and action steps are mutually derived to ensure client buy-in and commitment.

150. C: Treating underlying conditions cannot reverse cirrhosis. Cirrhosis is a condition resulting in scarring of the liver. Excessive alcohol consumption, viral infections, and fatty liver cause cirrhosis. Although medications can slow the progression of cirrhosis, there is currently no cure. Symptoms of cirrhosis include but are not limited to jaundice, nausea, decreased appetite, itchy skin, fatigue, and fluid buildup in the abdomen and legs. In addition, cirrhosis can be caused by hepatitis B and C and taking antiviral medication can slow its progression. Treating concurrent conditions, such as obesity and alcohol use, can also prevent cirrhosis from worsening.

Practice Test #2

1. Genetic factors can play a significant role in an individual's susceptibility to substance abuse and addiction. It is estimated that genetic factors account for

a. 20–40% of addiction vulnerability.
b. 30–50% of addiction vulnerability.
c. 40–60% of addiction vulnerability.
d. 50–70% of addiction vulnerability.

2. Which is MOST true of individuals voluntarily entering treatment for substance use disorder?

a. They are committed to change.
b. They are fully ready to change.
c. They are at varying stages of change readiness.
d. They are primarily in need of encouragement.

3. According to the DSM-5-TR, irritability, poor concentration, and anxiety are withdrawal symptoms for which one of the following?

a. PCP.
b. Inhalants.
c. Nicotine.
d. Hallucinogens.

4. When helping families adjust to and maintain in-home sobriety, what is the therapeutic intervention that draws upon extended support linkages to produce motivation and reinforcement known as?

a. Structural or strategic systems therapy
b. Network therapy
c. Cognitive-behavioral therapy
d. Multidimensional family therapy

5. Best practices in clinical documentation suggest that each session note must include which of the following?

a. Treatment progress.
b. Treatment adherence.
c. Treatment participation.
d. Treatment compliance.

6. The US Department of Health and Human Services (HHS) provides protections at covered entities for violations of all of the following EXCEPT:

a. civil rights.
b. equal pay.
c. religious freedom.
d. HIPAA privacy and security.

7. The capacity to be empathetic is important in counseling. What must a counselor do when relating to clients over issues of their past?

a. Avoid any kind of emotional connection that compromises objectivity.
b. Avoid becoming overly drawn into the client's history and issues.
c. Ensure total immersion in the client's issues to properly relate and understand.
d. Ensure every detail of past pain and trauma is relieved and released.

8. What is the purpose of screening?

a. To prepare the client for program admission
b. To determine client readiness for change
c. To establish client diagnoses and treatment needs
d. To determine the need for placement or referral

9. The Controlled Substances Act—Title II of the Comprehensive Drug Abuse Prevention and Control Act of 1970—provides classifications for all of the following substances EXCEPT:

a. alcohol.
b. marijuana.
c. anabolic steroids.
d. lysergic acid diethylamide (LSD).

10. Circumstances, Motivation, Readiness, and Suitability (CMRS) Scales are used for what purpose?

a. Assessing client readiness for treatment
b. Assessing various financial and family support domains
c. Assessing client suitability for research participation
d. Assessing clients for treatment level of care

11. The term "substance use trajectory" refers to:

a. individual substance use patterns over the lifespan
b. the rates at which a given substance enters the body
c. substance metabolism over time
d. behavioral patterns of intoxication

Refer to the following for questions 12-15:

The client is a 14-year-old non-Hispanic white transgender male enrolled in the 8th grade. The student receives school-based counseling for depression and anxiety. The client's parents attended the initial intake session and provided written authorization allowing the client to participate in therapy, and the client signed an assent form. The client, whose pronouns are they/them, reports being bullied by peers, having fleeting thoughts of suicide, and using marijuana weekly to reduce anxiety. The counselor has diagnosed the client with gender dysphoria and generalized anxiety disorder.

The client has begun to transition socially, as evidenced by a change of name, pronouns, and clothing consistent with their identified gender. This has been a gradual evolution, which began in the 6th grade after several years of wanting to transition. The process has been challenging and mainly hidden from their parents, who the client reports as being strict and religiously conservative. The client resists family therapy, feeling their parents do not understand them, and explains that they responded punitively during the client's initial transition. The client voices concern about their desire to begin the medical transition process and realizes that they will not have their parents' support.

The client has recently become despondent in response to antitrans legislation in the client's state, which allows teachers and administrators to refer to students by their gender assigned at birth and restrict which bathrooms students are permitted to use. As a result, the counselor has become increasingly concerned for the client's safety and seeks supervision to help establish an effective short-term crisis plan.

12. Which one of the following represents the greatest suicide risk factor(s) for the client?

a. Religious affiliation.
b. Parental control (i.e., authoritarian parenting style).
c. Marijuana use.
d. Stigma and discrimination.

13. The primary purpose of delivering gender-affirming care to young people is to:

a. assist transgender youth with attaining medical and/or surgical interventions.
b. reduce mental health disparities among transgender and nonbinary youth.
c. reduce gender dysphoria among cisgender and transgender youth.
d. promote equitable access to mental health services among gender-diverse populations.

14. What is the counselor's responsibility in disclosing a minor client's substance use to their parents?

a. The counselor has an ethical duty to warn the parents.
b. The counselor has an ethical duty to report substance use to the parent.
c. The counselor has an ethical duty to uphold the client's confidentiality.
d. The counselor has an ethical duty to encourage the client to disclose their substance use to their parents.

15. The counselor seeks a standardized screening instrument to determine whether the client is using other substances, and, if so, at what frequency in the past year. Which one of the following tools would best provide this information?

a. S2BI.
b. TAPS.
c. DAST-10.
d. CRAFFT.

16. Which one of the following is not an established twelve-step program?

a. Narcotics Anonymous
b. Cocaine Anonymous
c. Hallucinogens Anonymous
d. Alcoholics Anonymous

17. Which of the following medications is NOT commonly used in the treatment of opioid abuse?

a. Luminal
b. Methadone
c. Buprenorphine
d. Levo-alpha acetylmethadol

18. How many Assessment Dimensions are recognized by the American Society of Addiction Medicine (ASAM)?

a. Two assessment dimensions
b. Four assessment dimensions
c. Six assessment dimensions
d. Eight assessment dimensions

19. Which of the following is the MOST common characteristic of a psychedelic drug?

a. altered perception
b. depression
c. increased alertness
d. sleepiness

20. During the initial intake interview, clinicians using the ASAM dimensions to guide treatment must first determine which of the following?

a. The client's current stage of change.
b. The overall severity of the symptoms.
c. The presence of co-occurring disorders.
d. The client's ability to form a therapeutic alliance.

21. Which one of the following assesses a client's degree of assurance for handling relapse triggers?

a. Opioid Risk Tool – OUD.
b. Rosenburg Self-Esteem Scale.
c. Readiness to Change Questionnaire.
d. Situational Confidence Questionnaire.

22. The overarching goal of behavioral health equity is to provide access to affordable, high-quality services to:

a. reduce medical mistrust among under-resourced populations.
b. promote the use of evidence-based practices for all populations.
c. provide person-centered care for populations affected by inequality.
d. reduce persistent behavioral health disparities among affected populations.

23. Research shows that epigenetic factors make up roughly what proportion of the risk for substance use disorder?

a. Less than one-tenth
b. One-quarter
c. One-half
d. Three-quarters

Refer to the following for questions 24-27:

The client is a 48-year-old female who presents with a flat affect and a disheveled appearance. She explains that her 16-year-old daughter died unexpectedly nearly 2 years ago after having a grand mal seizure. The client states that moving forward has felt impossible and that she struggles with seeing other friends' children experience their proms, graduations, and other firsts.

Since her daughter's death, the client reports drinking more than she normally would. Six months ago, the client was charged with a driving under the influence (DUI) charge, with a blood alcohol concentration (BAC) of three times the legal limit. The client states that she drinks four to five glasses of wine nightly. She says that she was a social drinker before her daughter's death and relays that she initially increased her use to help with sleep. She admits to occasionally drinking in the mornings to "steady my nerves." The client is married, and no other children are in the home. Her husband has indicated that his wife has a drinking problem, but she minimizes his concerns, reporting that he has "checked out and buried himself in his work" since their daughter's death.

The client reports that her father died of alcoholism at 58 years old and that her mother has been diagnosed with bipolar disorder. She states that she has fleeting suicidal thoughts without a current plan and no prior attempts. The client has a history of migraine headaches and periodically takes prescription hydrocodone for pain. She sees a psychiatrist, who has prescribed lorazepam as needed for anxiety. She acknowledges the dangers of mixing medications with alcohol but explains that the situation is under control. The client freely provides a medical history but does not sign an authorization form allowing the counselor to communicate with her prescribers.

24. Given the information provided, which DSM diagnosis should be considered?

a. Substance misuse disorder.
b. Bipolar disorder.
c. Alcohol use disorder.
d. Substance-induced sleep disorder.

25. The client's prescription drug and alcohol use places her at high risk for harmful consequences. Does the counselor have an ethical obligation to contact her prescribers?

a. Yes, the client is mixing substances that act on the central nervous system, placing her in imminent danger.
b. No, the client did not provide authorization allowing the counselor to do so.
c. Yes, the client's fleeting suicidal ideation and substance use put her in imminent danger.
d. No, the client is not currently motivated to change her substance use patterns.

26. Alcohol impacts neurotransmitters by decreasing levels of which one of the following?

a. Dopamine.
b. Serotonin.
c. Gamma-aminobutyric acid.
d. Glutamate.

27. The counselor and client construct treatment plan goals and objectives. When discussing treatment modalities, they determine that the client would participate in a structured program with 16 hours of counseling per week for approximately 8–12 weeks. Which one of the following modalities would provide these services?

a. Brief therapy program.
b. Outpatient therapy program.
c. Intensive outpatient program.
d. Residential treatment program.

28. When asked about her pattern of drinking, a female client states, "I usually have four or five drinks if I'm out for a couple of hours, but this only happens once or twice a month." The client is engaging in:

a. binge drinking.
b. mild alcohol use.
c. moderate drinking.
d. heavy drinking.

29. Regarding advocating for the client diagnosed with substance or alcohol use disorder, which is true of case management?

a. The case manager can advocate with other service providers for a client's specific needs.
b. The case manager typically does not inform service providers of the client's diagnosis.
c. The case manager can never negotiate with any agency about their rules to help a client.
d. The case manager is legally unable to advocate sanctions from the criminal justice system.

30. Beneficence is to maleficence as autonomy is to:

a. competence.
b. coercion.
c. obedience.
d. justice.

31. What does the BIRP progress note acronym stand for?

a. Behavior, Interview, Reaction, Purpose
b. Behavior, Integrate, Review, Propose
c. Behavior, Intervention, Response, Plan
d. Behavior, Intervene, Revise, Program

32. What is the euphoria experienced when under the influence of cocaine caused by?

a. A cascade-effect of endorphins
b. A sudden release of adrenalin
c. Increased basal metabolic rate
d. A buildup of neurotransmitters

33. When a drug is ingested orally, which of the following BEST describes how the drug enters the bloodstream?

a. through the lungs.
b. through blood vessels.
c. through the small intestine.
d. through nasal membranes.

34. The treatment plan should be:

a. reflective of the client's level of care after the initial phase of treatment.
b. a collaborative effort between the client and counselor.
c. updated at six-month intervals.
d. generic and non-descript.

35. For the counselor, in which of the following is the influence of culture is MOST likely to be apparent?

a. Symptom presentation
b. Screening responses
c. Mental status examination
d. Substances used

36. Which one of the following statements is NOT true of risk factors?

a. Risk factors rarely occur in isolation.
b. Risk factors can be eliminated by protective factors.
c. Risk factors can exist among groups and individuals.
d. Risk factors are cumulative and co-occurring.

37. The racial mix of the United States continues to shift substantially. What is the fastest-growing minority group in the nation?

a. Hispanics and Latinos
b. Asians and Pacific Islanders
c. African Americans
d. Native Americans

38. The client states, "I just don't think alcohol is a problem for me." Which one of the following counselor responses is an example of an amplified reflection?

a. "On the one hand, you would like to stop drinking, but on the other hand, you think it is not a problem for you."
b. "There are absolutely no consequences associated with your alcohol use."
c. "You don't see a downside to your drinking, yet you received a driving under the influence charge."
d. "You really don't think alcohol is a problem for you."

39. During the process of evaluation and assessment, clinicians engage in all of the following EXCEPT:

a. ascertain any biomedical conditions or complications.
b. identify motivation or readiness to change.
c. determine the existence of substance use.
d. calculate the extent and severity of substance use.

40. The mnemonic SIGECAPS evaluates which psychological state?

a. Depression
b. Anxiety
c. Paranoia
d. Mania

41. Which of the following substances is MOST commonly implicated in suicidal deaths?

a. Methamphetamines.
b. Marijuana.
c. Cocaine.
d. Alcohol.

42. Twelve-step programs encourage individuals in early sobriety to change their usual people, places, and things as a means of breaking the chain of use. This situational specificity of substance use is referred to as:

a. cross-tolerance.
b. reverse tolerance.
c. conditioned tolerance.
d. dispositional tolerance.

43. According to the 2021 National Survey on Drug Use and Health (NSDUH), which of the following populations were LEAST likely to seek substance use disorder treatment?

a. Non-Hispanic whites.
b. Hispanics.
c. Black or African Americans.
d. American Indians and Alaska Natives.

44. Gender-affirming care is an individualized treatment for LBGT youth that includes the all of the following components EXCEPT:

a. developmentally appropriate psychoeducation regarding gender and sexuality.
b. evidence-based practices supporting reparative therapy for youth and families.
c. therapeutic interventions for use with gender dysphoria to eliminate or lessen the risk of poor mental health outcomes.
d. validating means of social transitioning for youth experiencing gender dysphoria (e.g., use of pronouns, name changes).

45. How many categories does SAMHSA's Service Coordination Framework for Co-Occurring Disorders have?

a. Two.
b. Four.
c. Six.
d. Eight.

46. Substance-induced disorders refer specifically to:

a. Poor occupational functioning resulting from substance use.
b. Dysfunctional family interactions secondary to substance use.
c. Psychiatric symptoms brought on by substance use.
d. Physical ailments brought on by substance use.

47. LSD affects sleep, mood, digestion, and body temperature due to interactions with which one of the following receptors?

a. Dopamine.
b. Serotonin.
c. Norepinephrine.
d. GABA.

48. Microaggressions are damaging to marginalized groups, primarily because they tend to be:

a. cumulative.
b. intentional.
c. confrontational.
d. explicit.

49. Opiates are obtained from which of the following?

a. Chemical compounds
b. Plant sources
c. Animal sources
d. Microbiological sources.

50. According to the American Society of Addiction Medicine (ASAM), which of the following is the highest level of care on a treatment continuum?

a. Medically Managed Intensive Inpatient services.
b. Intensive Inpatient services.
c. Withdrawal Management in a residential setting.
d. Residential/Inpatient services.

51. The term *double trouble*, in reference to mutual-help groups, refers to what?

a. Groups for clients with both psychiatric and substance abuse issues
b. Groups for clients with both legal and substance abuse issues
c. Groups for clients with polysubstance abuse concerns
d. Groups for clients with a personality disorder and substance abuse

52. How are the clinical, evaluative, and administrative activities that link clients with treatment, community services, and other resources needed to carry out a treatment plan MOST comprehensively referred to?

a. Case management
b. Client advocacy
c. Service coordination
d. Resource linkage

53. It is determined that a client requires tertiary prevention in the context of substance use disorder (SUD). Which of the following services would the client likely derive the most benefit from?

a. Participation in community-wide education on SUD and its consequences.
b. Outpatient treatment services for SUD.
c. Screening services to help determine if the client is at-risk for SUD.
d. Small group informational sessions to obtain resources for SUD.

54. Which of the following is NOT a "drug cue"?

a. A prior drug use setting
b. Drug use paraphernalia
c. Seeing others use drugs
d. Drug avoidance strategies

55. In one facet of relapse prevention therapy (RPT), the counselor helps the client to manage cravings, recognize early warnings of relapse, and reframe their reactions to a first lapse. This best describes which aspect of RPT?

a. assessment procedures
b. teaching cognitive coping skills
c. techniques to raise awareness
d. lifestyle modification strategies

56. What response to a drug has developed when increased dosages of the drug are required over time to achieve the same effect as the original dosage?

a. Tolerance
b. Dependence
c. Withdrawal
d. Toxicity

57. According the DSM-5-TR criteria, a client that has previously met the criteria for stimulant use disorder but now has not met the criteria for stimulant use in 10 months (except for craving) would be termed to be in _________ remission.

a. Full
b. Partial
c. Early
d. Sustained

Refer to the following for questions 58-61:

Rachel, a 17-year-old 11th-grader, is being treated at an inpatient facility for AUD. Before her admission, Rachel was charged with a DUI after crashing her car into a telephone pole. Although her car was totaled, there were no injuries. She was taken to the ED, where her BAC was registered at 0.17% g/dL.

Rachel is also diagnosed with major depressive disorder. She has had multiple suicide attempts and engages in risky sexual activities. Rachel endorses feeling sad daily and has become disinterested in activities that she once enjoyed. She has done well at the treatment center and plans to transition back home. Rachel's parents have received psychoeducation and now understand that addiction is a chronic, treatable disease. They have also learned to recognize the signs and symptoms of alcohol use, overdose, and withdrawal.

Today, she attends a family therapy session with her mother and father. Rachel has a twin brother, Richard, who could not attend today's session. Earlier in the week, Rachel felt anxious and on edge regarding her upcoming family therapy session. During the family session, she complains about the "unfair treatment" she receives compared to her brother, stating, "He drinks just as much as I do, and there are no consequences." The counselor redirects Rachel and uses motivational interviewing to reinforce her progress and commitment to change.

58. The American Society of Addiction Medicine (ASAM) defines addiction as a chronic, treatable disease involving complex interactions among all of the following EXCEPT:

a. genetics.
b. brain circuitry.
c. individual choice.
d. environmental factors.

59. Current data in alcohol use indicate gender-specific trends for girls and young women ages 12–20. Compared to boys and men in the same age range, girls and women have:

a. higher instances of alcohol use.
b. higher instances of societal acceptance surrounding alcohol use.
c. lower instances of drinking to cope with mental disorders.
d. lower BAC levels after consuming equal amounts of alcohol.

60. Symptoms of Rachel's co-occurring mental disorder include which one of the following?

a. Feeling on edge.
b. Poor concentration.
c. Argumentative behavior.
d. Risky alcohol use.

61. Rachel's parents have learned to recognize symptoms of alcohol toxicity (i.e., poisoning). Which symptom is commonly associated with alcohol toxicity?

a. Hyposomnia.
b. Hyperthermia.
c. Slurred speech.
d. Irregular breathing.

62. Which is true of substance induced mood disorders?

a. Symptoms of mood disorder most commonly occur during active use.
b. Symptoms of the mood disorder are less likely to resolve with abstinence.
c. Symptoms of mood disorder most widely occur with heavy alcohol use.
d. Symptoms of the mood disorder are less likely to mimic the corresponding mood disorder.

63. According to a National report on treatment court programs, the opioid epidemic is now coupled with a "co-existing epidemic of sorts" due to the rise in which of the following?

a. Nicotine use.
b. Marijuana use.
c. Alcohol use.
d. Stimulants use.

64. How is the individual who is responsible to carry out the clinical monitoring and collaborative client assessments, evaluations, referrals, treatment coordination, and goodness-of-fit appraisals of the treatment plan to client goals and objectives BEST known as?

a. Case manager
b. Service coordinator
c. Therapist
d. Administrator

65. Which of the following is the most commonly abused central nervous system depressant?

a. Benzodiazepines
b. Barbiturates
c. Alcohol
d. Opioids

66. What is the MOST common symptom of Wernicke's encephalopathy?

a. New memory formation
b. Loss of older memories
c. Psychosis
d. Confusion

67. Working with substance-abusing clients can result in a variety of emotive experiences. What does the term *secondary trauma* refer to?

a. The overlay of emotional abuse in a physically abusive relationship
b. The medical sequelae that may arise after years of emotional abuse
c. Entering a relationship with abusive features like those experienced before
d. Symptoms in the counselor emerging from high exposure to client traumas

68. To engage in advocacy, APs must understand the criminalization of SUD and its impact on communities of color. Of the following, which one is true?

a. Current laws in the United States reflect an understanding that addiction is a treatable medical disease.
b. America's war on drugs initiative was costly but effective in eliminating disparities in communities of color.
c. Current laws in the United States have punished violent and nonviolent drug offenders proportionately.
d. Current laws in the United States have perpetuated generational trauma and inequitable access to treatment in communities of color.

69. What does client resistance to treatment MOST likely indicate?

a. The client is being pressured to change too quickly.
b. The client simply does not care to overcome the problem.
c. The client has been coerced into treatment.
d. The client is embarrassed about past relapses.

70. Which of the following BEST describes the function of a release of information?

a. It allows the counselor to communicate confidential information to a specified party.
b. It gives the counselor the right to transfer client information whenever appropriate.
c. It allows the counselor to release client records to be used in court proceedings.
d. It protects identifiable health information from being released without client consent.

71. Which statement BEST reflects the nature of mutual-help groups such as twelve-step programs?

a. These programs vary greatly and should be carefully chosen.
b. These programs are generally very much the same.
c. These programs are only for substance abusers.
d. These programs are primarily religious in nature and orientation.

72. Housing First, an evidence-based practice for housing insecurity, is grounded in the principle of consumer:

a. choice.
b. sobriety.
c. nonmaleficence.
d. motivation to change.

73. During an initial intake assessment, counselors wishing to establish rapport and trust with a new client would first do which of the following?

a. Tell the client what you expect to accomplish in this session.
b. Ask the client's permission to address the subject of change.
c. Inform the client of the duration of this first session.
d. Tell the client what you expect to achieve in the long term.

74. Addiction causes neuroadaptation, which stimulates a strong urge to obtain and consume a substance when it is absent or discontinued. This process is known as:

a. craving.
b. relapse.
c. tolerance.
d. withdrawal.

75. Which of the following routes of administration is the quickest and most intense?

a. Oral.
b. Intravenous.
c. Nasal.
d. Rectal.

76. Compared to adults of all ages, which is true of rates of illicit drug use and co-occurring disorders among older adults?

a. Rates of illicit drug use are steadily increasing, while rates of co-occurring mental disorders are also high.
b. Rates of illicit drug use are steadily decreasing, while rates of co-occurring mental disorders are also low.
c. Rates of illicit drug use remain stable, while rates of co-occurring mental disorders are high.
d. Rates of illicit drug use are low, while rates of co-occurring mental disorders are high.

77. Which of the following is NOT measured by the DIS schedule?

a. Substance use disorders
b. Alcohol use disorders
c. Psychiatric disorders
d. Physical health disorders

78. Which one of the following is classified as a non-substance-related disorder in the DSM-5-TR?

a. Caffeine use disorder.
b. Gambling disorder.
c. Internet gaming disorder.
d. Compulsive shopping disorder.

79. Which one of the following forms of bias involves selectively organizing information to validate preexisting beliefs and ideas?

a. Affinity bias.
b. Confirmation bias.
c. Conformity bias.
d. Attribution bias.

80. How is the concept of resilience, from the perspective of mental health, BEST described?

a. Internal strengths necessary to cope with challenging events
b. Adequate resources to draw upon in times of emotional compromise
c. Social networks that can offer support during times of distress
d. Intellectual fund of information to reason and cope well with problems

81. How many main levels exist in the substance abuse continuum of care, according to the American Society of Addiction Medicine (ASAM)?

a. Three levels of care
b. Four levels of care
c. Five levels of care
d. Six levels of care

82. What does the acronym GATE stand for?

a. Gather information; Access supervision; Take responsible action; Extend the action
b. Gather resources; Access procedures; Take clinical notes; Extend the intervention
c. Gather documentation; Access contacts; Take counsel; Extend positive outcomes
d. Gather evidence; Access records; Take consultation; Extend documentation

83. Empathy refers to a counselor's ability to:

a. feel what the client is feeling.
b. understand what the client is experiencing.
c. show sympathy for the client.
d. change unproductive feelings.

84. Which one of the following statements is NOT true of addiction?

a. It can be treated.
b. It can be prevented.
c. It permanently changes brain chemistry.
d. It requires ongoing monitoring and support for recovery.

85. What is/are the organ(s) most damaged by cocaine use?

a. The brain
b. The lungs
c. The kidneys
d. The heart

86. What should the position of treatment programs toward twelve-step programs be?

a. Clients should not be discouraged from twelve-step programs.
b. Clients should be encouraged to participate in twelve-step programs.
c. Twelve-step programs are a helpful social tool but have no other impact.
d. Twelve-step programs are an integral part of overall client success.

87. APs ensure clients' records are securely stored, maintained, and protected against unauthorized persons. APs provide this information during:

a. duty to warn.
b. informed consent.
c. the initial intake interview.
d. the review of client rights.

88. Cognitive-behavioral therapy (CBT) does NOT address which of the following?

a. Replacing substance abuse coping with more effective coping skills
b. Identifying personal cues or triggers that lead to substance abuse
c. Learning new problem-solving skills and strategies to counteract substance abuse urges
d. The role of a higher power in achieving and maintaining abstinence

89. Which of the following is NOT a type of intensive outpatient treatment (IOT) group?

a. Psychoeducational groups
b. Skills development groups
c. Interpersonal process groups
d. Transitional care groups

Refer to the following for questions 90-93:

Lee, a newly certified addiction professional (AP), works at an outpatient treatment center for adolescents with substance use disorder (SUD). Lee grew up in an abusive home and is estranged from his biological family. As a teenager, Lee struggled with feelings of inferiority and used substances to cope. He is now sober and has been employed with the agency for more than 1 year. Lee is required to manage a full caseload and meet productivity standards.

In the past few months, Lee has come to work late and called in sick multiple times. He is exhausted and feels physically ill when arriving to his office building. He conducts group therapy three times weekly and explains to his supervisor that the group is ineffective and disruptive. His supervisor is dismissive and reiterates that providing group therapy is an expectation for all APs. Lee is reminded that he has multiple deficient case notes and has failed to meet his productivity requirements. Lee is placed on a performance improvement plan. He voices that he feels he has been treated unfairly and notices familiar feelings of inadequacy and inferiority resurfacing.

Later that day, Lee meets with his client Marcus. He learns that Marcus continues to skip school, use substances, and is habitually truant. Lee believes that this client has had no real repercussions for his actions and becomes visibly angry. He finds himself fighting back tears and begins to lecture Marcus on the value of his education. He tells Marcus that, unlike himself, he has parents in his life who actually care.

In another session, Lee meets with Jada, a 14-year-old client whose parents are in a custody battle. Jada, who lives with her mother, asks Lee if he can keep a secret. She tells Lee that she is having sex with a 22-year-old in the neighborhood. She begs him not to tell her parents because she worries that she will then have to live with her abusive father. He assures her he will keep the information confidential. Jada is relieved and hugs Lee as she leaves. Believing that the disclosure could potentially harm his client, Lee does not document their discussion. As time progresses, Lee is unable to meet his supervisor's expectations and eventually becomes apathetic and detached from his clients.

90. Maslach and Jackson's multidimensional theory of burnout consists of three components. Lee's burnout is evidenced by which one of these components?

a. Vicarious trauma.
b. Emotional exhaustion.
c. Lack of professional support.
d. Overidentification with clients.

91. Lee's reaction to Marcus exemplifies which one of the following?

a. Transference.
b. Triangulation.
c. Countertransference.
d. Secondary traumatization.

92. Lee's interaction with Jada is most likely an example of a(n):

a. boundary crossing.
b. blurred boundary.
c. boundary violation.
d. enmeshed boundary.

93. Lee agrees to keep Jada's sexual relationship confidential and does not document their conversation. According to the NAADAC Code of Ethics (2021), Lee's actions are most likely:

a. ethical because the disclosure could cause Jada to have to live with her abusive father, placing her in imminent danger.
b. unethical because a treatment summary can be provided if full access to the client's records proves harmful.
c. ethical because APs must protect the confidentiality of minor clients who lack the capacity to provide voluntary informed consent.
d. unethical because the AP's performance improvement plan is evidence of the AP practicing outside his scope of practice.

94. Which one of the following statements is true regarding cocaine use?

a. The euphoria from smoking crack cocaine lasts between 8 and 12 hours.
b. Nearly half of ingested cocaine is excreted in urine within 1 hour.
c. The euphoria from snorting powder cocaine is more intense than smoking crack cocaine.
d. Acute intoxication is characterized by dysphoria, agitation, and anxiety.

95. Which one of the following prescreening instruments consists of three questions related to the frequency and quantity of alcohol use?

a. Alcohol Use Disorders Identification Test.
b. Global Appraisal of Individual Needs Short Screener.
c. Drug Abuse Screen Test-1 (DAST-1).
d. Brief Screener for Tobacco, Alcohol, and Other Drugs.

96. Which one of the following is a four-item questionnaire that asks about suicidal ideation in one's lifetime and within the past year, the present threat of suicide, and the likelihood of suicidal acts in the future?

a. Columbia–Suicide Severity Rating Scale.
b. DSM-5 Self-Rated Level 1 Cross-Cutting Symptom Measure.
c. Mental Health Screening Form-III.
d. Suicide Behaviors Questionnaire-Revised.

97. To date, there are over one million Americans living with HIV. Approximately what percentage of cases are found among females in this country?

a. 5 percent
b. 15 percent
c. 25 percent
d. 35 percent

98. A potential client enters a program for treatment and a counselor recognizes him from a Little League team in which their sons are both still active. What is the BEST response by the counselor?

a. Pretend to have not seen the acquaintance, and never speak of it to them.
b. Speak with the client privately, and offer assurances of confidentiality.
c. Seek to be assigned as the client's counselor to ease tension and show support.
d. Refer the client to another treatment program.

99. What is the primary reason that ordered and routine activities are built into the therapeutic community (TC) treatment process?

a. To aid in level of care transitions.
b. To establish structure and predictability.
c. To earn community privileges.
d. To create a social hierarchy.

100. A functional analysis of substance use typically includes:

a. An investigation into a person's lessened response to a substance.
b. An assessment of a person's threshold for substance dependency.
c. An examination into a person's triggers and consequences of substance use.
d. A look into a person's behaviors that interfere with their basic needs.

101. How many treatment weeks are involved in the current Matrix Model program?

a. Twelve weeks
b. Sixteen weeks
c. Twenty-four weeks
d. Thirty-two weeks

102. Which of the following MOST properly defines screening and assessment?

a. Screening evaluates a problem; assessment diagnoses it.
b. Screening identifies a problem; assessment treats it
c. Screening looks for a problem; assessment defines it.
d. Screening reveals a problem; assessment resolves it.

103. What is the purpose of open-ended heterogeneous groups?

a. To allow flexibility in new member assignments
b. To keep difficult clients away from each other
c. To put clients together with similar issues
d. To meet the needs of clients with special problems

104. The mnemonic DIG-FAST evaluates which psychological state?

a. Depression
b. Anxiety
c. Paranoia
d. Mania

105. What is the key difference between a treatment plan and a progress note?

a. The treatment plan evaluates client achievements, while a progress note ensures action steps are taken to meet objectives.
b. The treatment plan addresses client needs, while a progress note specifies service providers' interventions.
c. The treatment plan records events and activities, while a progress note captures the client's current clinical presentation.
d. The treatment plan provides an action blueprint, while the progress note captures each clinical exchange.

106. Marijuana is eliminated from the body mainly via...

a. urine.
b. feces.
c. vomiting.
d. sweating.

107. Fundamental ethical principles govern the addiction treatment process, especially in situations of medication-assisted treatment (MAT) for opioid addiction. What does the principle of nonmaleficence refer to?

a. Preserving client autonomy
b. Working to a client's benefit
c. Doing no harm to a client
d. Faithfully honoring commitments

108. Research indicates that societal stigma surrounding treatment for opioid use disorder (OUD) can be mitigated through which one of the following?

a. Needle exchange programs.
b. Integrated behavioral health care.
c. Lesser penalties for nonviolent offenders.
d. Improving access to homeless shelters.

109. Telescoping is a term used to describe substance use disparities according to which one of the following?

a. Age.
b. Gender.
c. Ethnicity.
d. Sexual orientation.

110. Which of the following developmental stages are individuals MOST likely to develop a problem with substance use?

a. Middle age
b. Young adulthood
c. Adolescence
d. Childhood

111. Principle III-39 of the NAADAC Code of Ethics (2021) addresses client referrals, stating that APs shall NOT:

a. accept referrals from professionals with whom they have engaged in a romantic, sexual, social, or familial relationship.
b. refer clients from their places of employment to their private practice without prior documented authorization.
c. accept referrals from colleagues to accommodate service interruptions without client authorization.
d. refer clients to professionals with whom there is no previously established professional relationship.

112. Which one of the following is a four-item outcomes measure administered at the beginning of each session to assess treatment progress?

a. Health of the Nation Outcome Scales.
b. Outcome Questionnaire.
c. Outcome Rating Scale.
d. Daily Living Activities.

113. Which one of the following psychoactive substances can be classified as a depressant, stimulant, or hallucinogen?

a. MDMA.
b. LSD.
c. Ketamine.
d. Marijuana.

114. The Health Insurance Portability and Accountability Act of 1986 Privacy Rule offers federal protections for covered entities, allowing client access to their personal health information EXCEPT for their:

a. functional status.
b. collateral notes.
c. psychotherapy notes.
d. treatment plans.

115. Which is true of the human immunodeficiency virus (HIV)?

a. HIV is transmitted either intravenously or sexually.
b. HIV can be cured with antiretroviral therapy (ART).
c. HIV cannot be transmitted through coughing or sneezing.
d. HIV is more common in older adults than in the general population.

116. Optimal group size in a typical treatment group involves how many members?

a. 8–15 members
b. 6–12 members
c. 5–10 members
d. 4–8 members

117. What does the Treatment Services Review (TSR-6) assessment instrument measure?

a. Therapeutic intensity and problem severity
b. Solution-oriented therapeutic resistance
c. Nature and intensity of treatment services
d. Topic-specific remedial outcomes

Refer to the following for questions 118-121:

Debra is a 22-year-old female residing in a rural community. She receives therapy from Cheryl, an AP who is in long-term sobriety herself. You have recently been hired to serve as Cheryl's clinical supervisor and are reviewing her cases.

You note that Cheryl initially provided in-person therapy to Debra but recently switched to video-based e-therapy due to Debra's inability to find childcare. Debra has recently regained custody of her children, ages 4 and 6, both of whom were removed for neglect.

Debra is diagnosed with attention deficit hyperactivity disorder (ADHD). The progress notes indicate that she began taking a prescription amphetamine 2 years ago. Debra took the medication as prescribed until a prolonged national shortage prevented her from consistently receiving her medication. Debra began using alternative methods of administration to improve efficacy. She started purchasing the substance illegally and later began selling it to support her chronic use. She was arrested for possessing illegal amphetamines and served 9 months in jail. The social worker at the jail referred Debra to Cheryl to assist her with efforts to regain custody of her children and address her concerns of worry, anxiety, and poor concentration.

During her weekly e-therapy sessions, Debra is distracted by her children's interruptions and often has to ask Cheryl to repeat her questions. Cheryl notes that her poor concentration is likely attributed to the lack of ADHD medication and refers Cheryl to a psychiatrist. Cheryl's weekly sessions include updates on the children's adjustment and a review of relapse prevention strategies. She reports that she can be short tempered and irritable with her children. She explains that this is complicated by sleepless nights and worry over finding a job and maintaining her sobriety. Debra has previously refused to attend 12-step meetings; however, Cheryl eventually persuaded her to attend. In the next session, Debra asks Cheryl to be her temporary sponsor due to the limited options afforded by their rural community.

118. Cheryl has been asked to serve as Debra's temporary sponsor. What is Cheryl's best course of action?

a. Decline the role and provide information on alternatives.
b. Accept the temporary role and establish a firm endpoint.
c. Decline the role and provide step work during therapy sessions.
d. Accept the role due to limited options for 12-step meetings.

119. How would you best instruct Cheryl to develop a medically necessary treatment plan?

a. Collaborate with Debra and prioritize any unresolved problems.
b. Seek consultation from a child abuse specialist.
c. Conduct a thorough biopsychosocial assessment.
d. Provide a screening, brief intervention, and referral to treatment.

120. Which one of the following is the primary challenge in using e-delivery with Debra?

a. Honoring client autonomy.
b. Maintaining confidentiality.
c. Developing a therapeutic alliance.
d. Delivering evidence-based practices.

121. Given Debra's symptoms and history, which of the following diagnoses warrants consideration as a differential diagnosis for ADHD?

a. Major depressive disorder
b. Post-traumatic stress disorder.
c. Oppositional defiant disorder.
d. Anxiety disorder.

122. Chronic and prolonged use of marijuana among adolescents is associated with which one of the following?

a. Malnourishment.
b. Heart damage.
c. Cognitive impairment (a lowered IQ).
d. Slurred speech.

123. The counselor-client relationship can be very complex. What does the term *transference* refer to?

a. Feelings from the client that the counselor uses to strengthen the relationship
b. Feelings from the counselor that the client accepts to grow and improve
c. Feelings from a past relationship that are projected onto the counselor
d. Feelings from current relationships that are added to the counseling experience

124. In which of the following stages of change would counselors intervene by providing clients with a menu of options?

a. Precontemplation.
b. Contemplation.
c. Preparation.
d. Action.

125. According to the integrated developmental model of supervision, a counselor's professional development is measured in of all of the following areas EXCEPT:

a. awareness.
b. motivation.
c. autonomy.
d. genuineness.

126. Which of the following substances are MOST harmful to fetal development?

a. Marijuana.
b. Amphetamines.
c. Alcohol.
d. Methadone.

127. What is the primary purpose of a substance use assessment?

a. To determine current level of functioning.
b. To identify precipitating factors.
c. To provide a diagnosis.
d. To assess the severity of substance use.

128. What does the NAADAC Code of Ethics (2021) say about addiction professionals (APs) and sexual relationships?

a. APs should not engage in a sexual relationship with a current or former client.
b. APs should not engage in a sexual relationship with a current client or former client for two years from service termination.
c. APs should not engage in a sexual relationship with a current client or former client for two years from service termination unless the relationship is deemed non-exploitative.
d. APs should not engage in a sexual relationship with a current client and are discouraged from engaging in a sexual relationship with a past client unless the relationship is deemed non-exploitative.

129. How is the CRAFT program or approach BEST described?

a. A consensus approach to motivating a client into treatment
b. A confrontational approach to motivating a client into treatment
c. A community or family approach to motivating a client into treatment
d. A consciousness-raising approach to motivating a client into treatment

130. For the process of case management to be culturally sensitive to ethnicity, race, disability, gender, sexual orientation, age, and other forms of client diversity, a case manager must understand the dynamics of interactions in cultural contexts. In addition, which of these is true?

a. The case manager need not acknowledge diversity but must be aware of its existence.
b. The case manager's respect for cultural diversity precludes cultural knowledge.
c. The case manager must do cultural self-assessment to be culturally competent.
d. The case manager can use the same practices regardless of a setting's diversity.

131. Substance abuse prevention for youth in school and community settings consists of all of the following EXCEPT

a. Universal programs
b. Selective programs
c. Indicated programs
d. Targeted programs

132. The DSM-5-TR provides four groupings of criteria for substance use disorder (SUD). Which one of the following groups includes intense and periodic cravings?

a. Risky use.
b. Social impairment.
c. Pharmacological criteria.
d. Impaired control over use.

133. What is a brief, but comprehensively integrated public health approach to early substance abuse intervention and treatment known as?

a. Treatment, Brief Intervention, Referral, and Screening (TBIRS)
b. Brief Intervention, Screening, Referral, and Treatment (BISRT)
c. Referral, Screening, Brief Intervention, and Treatment (RSBIT)
d. Screening, Brief Intervention, and Referral to Treatment (SBIRT)

134. Which is true of barbiturates?

a. Barbiturates are non-addictive when used as prescribed.
b. Barbiturates have a wide therapeutic index (i.e., therapeutic threshold).
c. Barbiturates carry an increased risk of psychological dependence when taken for sleep.
d. Barbiturates can cause psychological dependence when higher doses are taken daily for three months.

Refer to the following for questions 135-138:

Anthony is a 13-year-old 8th-grader referred by his school counselor for a drug and alcohol assessment. Today, he arrives at the intake session with his father, a single parent raising Anthony and his younger sister. Anthony's biopsychosocial assessment reveals that he was diagnosed with ADHD at age 8. His family doctor diagnosed Anthony and prescribed methylphenidate. Anthony's father was against medication at the time and believed he needed more discipline instead. School records indicate that the local child protective services agency was called for suspected physical abuse, but no reports were substantiated. Anthony's mother is in jail for drug-related charges. His father expressed concern that ADHD medication would be risky for Anthony because of his family history.

Anthony said he began sneaking alcohol at home in the 3rd or 4th grade. During this time, he also started smoking cigarettes and vaping nicotine. When asked about current substance use, he states, "Sometimes I do whippets or K2 with my friends. But mostly we just drink beer or smoke weed." Anthony reports that he continues to use substances despite his father's threats to "send me to juvie" and a steep decline in academic performance. Anthony is cutting class, associates with known neighborhood gang members, and downplays his substance use. He meets the criteria for conduct disorder because he has been repetitively aggressive toward others and was caught vandalizing school property and stealing from convenience stores. Anthony states that he can go for a while without using, but when he is out in the neighborhood, he experiences cravings that are difficult to resist.

135. Anthony reports using all of the following substances EXCEPT:

a. spice.
b. inhalants.
c. marijuana.
d. ketamine.

136. Empirical evidence supports which one of the following statements?

a. ADHD medication is a gateway drug to other substances.
b. Higher doses of stimulant medications are addictive.
c. There is a correlational relationship between ADHD and SUD.
d. There is a correlational relationship between taking ADHD medication and SUD.

137. Which area of an adolescent's brain is still developing, making them more susceptible to substance use?

a. The cerebellum.
b. The nucleus accumbens.
c. The prefrontal cortex.
d. The amygdala.

138. Which one of the following neurotransmitters is primarily responsible for providing individuals with the motivation to engage in substance use?

a. Dopamine.
b. Gamma-aminobutyric acid.
c. Norepinephrine.
d. Serotonin.

139. During the initial treatment phase, how many therapeutic contact hours per week does the American Society of Addiction Medicine (ASAM) require for intensive outpatient treatment (IOT) participants?

a. Three hours
b. Five hours
c. Seven hours
d. Nine hours

140. Of the following symptoms, which is most typical of intoxication with alcohol, tranquilizers, and opioids, but not with amphetamines?

a. low blood pressure
b. ataxia
c. disinhibition
d. nystagmus

141. Which of the following is the most accurate statement about case management?

a. It consists of a process of referrals to independent agencies.
b. It gives clients continuity by providing a single contact point.
c. It gives responsibility for multiservice clients to all agencies.
d. It means the case manager's obligation is only to the client.

142. What kind of drug does the term *nootropic* refer to?

a. Memory enhancing
b. Mood stabilizing
c. Hallucinogenic
d. Psychedelic

143. The term "homeostasis" in family therapy is best defined as:

a. The inability to sustain balanced relationships
b. Dynamic tension between opposing family members
c. The designation of family roles
d. Family balance through equilibrium

144. Harm reduction strategies are most effective for all of the following conditions EXCEPT:

a. HIV.
b. viral hepatitis.
c. self-injurious behaviors.
d. OUD.

145. Which of the following provides the highest confidentiality protection for clients with co-occurring disorders?

a. HIPAA.
b. 42 CFR Part 2.
c. PL 94-142.
d. Section 504.

146. Physical dependence on psychoactive substance is determined by which of the following?

a. The addictive properties of the substance.
b. The symptoms of withdrawal when the substance is reduced.
c. A persistent need to continue substance use.
d. The frequency and amount of the substance taken.

147. The Matrix Model is designed to treat the use of which of the following?

a. Stimulants
b. Alcohol
c. Barbiturates
d. Inhalants

148. The Food and Drug Administration (FDA) has approved medication assisted therapy for which of the following?

a. Hallucinogen disorder.
b. Cocaine use disorder.
c. Opioid use disorder.
d. Marijuana use disorder.

149. Substance-abusing clients can be clinically and personally challenging. Of what is compassion fatigue a key symptom?

a. Counselor burnout
b. Clients with high-abuse histories
c. Counselor apathy
d. Clients with multimodal issues

150. Clinicians working with clients in treatment for substance use disorder, must be aware of the applicable guidelines in 42 CFR Part 2. These guidelines refer to which of the following?

a. Substance abuse treatment program accreditation and standards
b. Issues involving the manufacture and sale of illicit drugs
c. Confidentiality in areas of alcohol and substance use disorder
d. Mandated client treatment under a court directive or order

Answer Key and Explanations for Test #2

1. C: While no single factor can account for all vulnerability, genetics appears to play a significant role. Other potential factors include gender, development stage, social environment, and culture or ethnicity. Known environmental risk factors include: unemployment or underemployment, high neighborhood crime rates, prevalence of illicit drugs (including cost and ease of procurement), poor housing (dilapidated or overcrowded), peer pressures, community attitudes, and low social achievement expectations. Known cultural or ethnic/racial risk factors include: minority status, discrimination based on race, intergenerational assimilation disparity, language and cultural barriers to social services and health care, poor educational achievement, cultural devaluation in the dominant society, and cultural alienation. Known family risk factors include: poor bonding, highly chaotic home, family conflict and violence, financial strain, home stress, parental substance abuse, parental neglect, and parental mental illness. Known emotional or behavioral risk factors include: low self-esteem, aggression, rebelliousness, high independence needs, nonconformity, shyness, delinquency, emotional problems, suicidality, relationship problems, using gateway drugs, and academic and drop-out problems.

2. C: Individuals present for treatment for a great variety of reasons. Among these are: (1) a need for transient relief from the effects of their substance use while still intending to return; (2) a primary desire to maintain employment, a marriage, physical health, mental health, or for other situationally driven reasons; (3) a desire to modify their substance use but recognizing only mildly associated problems;(4) ambivalent feelings about their substance use and unsure what they really want; (5) a genuine desire to change but with a sense of fear that they will be unable to produce the commitment needed to fully realize it; (6) a genuine desire to change patterns of substance use and a desire to stay sober. Determining where client readiness for change is crucial to producing a treatment approach that can optimize his or her potential for ultimate success.

3. C: Nicotine withdrawal is characterized by irritability, poor concentration, and anxiety. The DSM-5-TR does recognize withdrawal symptoms for phencyclidine (PCP), inhalants, and hallucinogens.

4. B: Network therapy builds an extended collection of involved persons (social workers, school counselors, legal representatives, therapists, etc.) to meet, motivate, and reinforce changes and progress in the family. Extensive interviews help determine family needs and appropriate referrals to resources such as support groups, counseling, and so on, to help break the cycle of addiction. Other therapeutic options include: (1) Multidimensional family therapy uses support groups, interviews, and therapeutic interactions to discover issues, map out responses, and contract with involved family members to address, curtail, or resolve key family issues. New family skills, such as better communication and conflict resolution, relapse prevention, and coping strategies for any psychiatric disorders in the family, are all needed for enhanced family functioning. (2) Cognitive-behavioral family therapy uses factual constructs, improved communication and negotiation skills, contingency contracting, and better problem definitions to produce enhanced family functioning. (3) Structural or strategic systems therapy restructures roles, realigns subsystems and boundaries, and reestablishes more extended intergenerational boundaries to improve family function and cohesion.

5. A: Best practices for clinical documentation suggest that treatment progress should be documented each session. Progress notes include the client's response to the AP's intervention, which is tied to the client's treatment plan goals, objectives, and interventions. Documenting treatment progress also aids in providing sound clinical decisions, continuity of care, and justifying claims to third party payers. Treatment adherence and compliance, including no-shows and cancellations, are generally recorded in an information note. Providing information on treatment participation is limited because it does not indicate how the client responded to the intervention and whether their participation relates to their treatment progress.

6. B: The US Department of Health and Human Services (HHS) provides protections at covered entities for violations of civil rights, religious freedom, and HIPAA privacy and security. The Equal Employment Opportunity Commission (EEOC) provides protections for job discrimination. Examples of EEOC covered protections include the Equal Pay Act of 1963 (EPA), the Americans with Disabilities Act (Title I and Title V), and the Civil Rights Act of 1964 (Title VII). HHS protects individuals from discriminatory practices for covered health and social service entities (including institutions and personnel), some of which may include hospitals, family health centers, Medicaid and Medicare providers, foster care agencies and homes, and homeless shelters. Civil rights laws protect individuals from discrimination due to race, age, sex, nationality, color, or disability. The Federal Conscience and Religious Freedom Laws help to protect individuals from "coercion, discrimination on the basis of conscience or religion, and burdens on the free exercise of religion." Lastly, HHS protects patient health information under the HIPAA Privacy Rule and the HIPAA Security Rule.

7. B: While empathy is important, it is necessary to find balance in working with clients who have suffered considerable past trauma and abuse. Becoming overly drawn in can cause the counselor to lose objectivity, become inappropriately emotional (angry, vengeful, etc.), and miss the opportunities to help the client move through and past his or her painful history. This can be particularly problematic if the counselor shares a similar past, which may easily lend to over-involvement in the presenting issues. In like manner, it also important that the counselor not be too dispassionate and detached, failing to allow the client to emotionally vent and unburden him- or herself. Typically, however, it is not necessary for a client to be prodded into revealing his or her past in minute detail. Rather, proper disclosure to the level needed for understanding is all that is necessary. It is important for counselors not to assume abuse from every symptom. As abuse in common in substance abusers, it is easy to infer abuse where it did not exist—especially with clients who are overly eager to please their counselor.

8. D: Screening aims to methodically review a client's presenting circumstances to determine the appropriateness (or lack thereof) for placement or further assessment and evaluation referral. Screening tools are also used to identify the presence or absence of mental disorders and/or a co-occurring substance use disorder. Screening tools do not attempt to diagnose a presenting co-occurring disorder but establish the likelihood of one being present. For clients who meet the criteria for further treatment, a referral is made to the program or individual who best matches the client's current needs. Once a complete evaluation is performed, a case conceptualization is formulated, which addresses the client's diagnosis, readiness for change, and treatment needs.

9. A: The Controlled Substances Act—Title II of the Comprehensive Drug Abuse Prevention and Control Act of 1970—does not classify or regulate alcohol. Title II created a scheduling system to classify substances according to their medical use, safety, and potential for abuse. Although marijuana is legal in some states, it is a schedule I substance due to the high potential for abuse and no currently accepted federal use. Anabolic steroids do not have psychoactive properties; however, they are a schedule III substance with medical use for breast cancer, hormone treatment, and low red blood cell count. Lysergic acid diethylamide (LSD) is a schedule I substance with no medical use and a high potential for abuse.

10. A: CMRS scales, by G. De Leon, were developed to aid in determining client readiness for substance abuse treatment. The scales measure client perceptions in four interrelated domains: circumstances (the external pressures influencing substance abuse change), motivation (internal pressures driving change), readiness (perception and acceptance of the need for treatment), and suitability (the client's perception of the appropriateness of the treatment modality or setting) for community or residential treatment. CMRS scales consist of eighteen Likert-type (five-point, strongly disagree to strongly agree) response items. The scores are summed to derive a total score. Research on validity and reliability has offered strong support for the CMRS scales.

11. A: Drug use trajectory refers to individual drug use patterns throughout one's lifespan. Lifespan research suggests that substance use has multiple origins, changes, and transitions arising from related biological, psychological, and social factors. For that reason, drug use research extends from embryological genetics through the development of personality, developmental change, and sociocultural and psychological influences. In addition, the interaction of genetics and environmental factors (i.e., epigenetics) are strong determinants of a person's risk of addiction.

12. D: Risk factors are cumulative and exist in multiple contexts. Stigma and discrimination are this client's greatest suicide risk factors because they occur in their social, family, school, and religious settings. Gender minority youth experience more instances of substance use and mental disorders, with minority stress cited as a strong contributor. Factors leading to minority stress include nonaffirming legislative actions, negative social attitudes, bullying, rejection from family members, and navigating environments that are not safe or affirming. Although conservative religious attitudes and beliefs can be harmful, religion is complex and nuanced, with supportive theology serving as a protective factor for gender-diverse youth. Children with authoritarian parents fare worse than those with parents who show warmth and support, particularly around the coming out process; however, the cumulative effect of interpersonal victimization and institutional discrimination in multiple contexts produces the greatest harm (e.g., internalized homonegativity). Lastly, while concerning, the client using marijuana to decrease anxiety does not outweigh the cumulative risk factors.

13. B: The primary purpose of delivering gender-affirming care to young people is to reduce mental health disparities among transgender and nonbinary youth. Gender-affirming care is highly individualized and provides targeted treatment to reduce mental and behavioral health disparities among individuals whose gender identity does not conform to their sex assigned at birth (i.e., transgender) and individuals whose concept of gender identity is not solely male or female (i.e., nonbinary). Practitioners who deliver gender-affirming care seek to reduce the effects of gender dysphoria by providing developmentally appropriate and gender-affirming interventions, including psychoeducation, social support, family therapy, and medical interventions. Not all gender-affirming care involves medical or surgical transitioning, with only a small fraction of transgender youth seeking those services. Gender dysphoria is absent in cisgender populations or in those whose gender identity conforms with the gender assigned at their birth. Lastly, although it is appropriate, promoting equitable access to mental health services among gender-diverse populations is not the primary purpose of gender-affirming care.

14. C: Principle II-17 of the NAADAC (the Association for Addiction Professionals) Code of Ethics (2021) states that APs are to protect the confidentiality of any information received when counseling minor children, and parents should be informed of the confidentiality limitations during the informed consent process. The parents provided written authorization allowing the client to participate in therapy, and the client signed an assent form indicating that confidentiality and informed consent were reviewed. Principle II-8 of the code addresses limitations to confidentiality, with exceptions including clients who are "a clear and imminent danger to themselves or to another person," which would exclude substance use. The duty to warn involves situations in which the client is a danger to another person. Although there are certain circumstances in which a counselor would encourage clients to disclose substance use to parents, in this situation, disclosure would likely conflict with the ethical principle of nonmaleficence because a lack of parental support is a significant stressor.

15. A: The Screening to Brief Intervention (S2BI) tool is used to determine a client's substance use and the frequency of substances used. The S2BI is appropriate for use with adolescents and determines the level of risk by asking the client about how many days in the past year they have used tobacco, marijuana, alcohol, inhalants, illicit drugs (e.g., cocaine, ecstasy), synthetic drugs (e.g., K2, spice), and prescription medications not prescribed to the client. The Tobacco, Alcohol, Prescription Medication, and Other Substance Use (TAPS) tool and the Drug Abuse Screen Test (DAST-10) are designed for adults and are not approved for use with adolescents. CRAFFT is approved for adolescents and screens teens for high-risk alcohol and other drug use disorders by asking questions related to the acronym CRAFFT (which stands for car, relax, forget, friends, trouble).

16. C: There is no twelve-step group for hallucinogen abuse, probably because, other than PCP, hallucinogens do not produce a withdrawal syndrome. Participation in community twelve-step and other mutual-help groups is an important part of the treatment process. Clients should understand that there are numerous program formats. For example, there are step meetings, open speaker meetings, and open and closed discussion meetings. Further, there are specialized groups such as those for women, for the hearing impaired, for the LGBT communities, for race and ethnicity groups, and for language-specific groups. Finally, for those less comfortable with a twelve-step approach, there are alternatives such as self-management and recovery training, secular organizations for sobriety, and Save Our Selves—which all use a twelve-step-like process to promote individual empowerment, self-determination, and self-affirmation.

17. A: Luminal is a barbiturate with no opioid management role. Opioid use disorder is very difficult to treat. Detoxification is insufficient, and relapse is common. Consequently, many clients may need maintenance on opioid substitutes that still enable them to function productively. These substitutes include methadone, buprenorphine (Subutex), and joint buprenorphine and naloxone preparations (sublingual Suboxone film and Zubsolv tablets). If crushed and injected, the naloxone precipitates opioid withdrawal but with no such effect sublingually. Frequently, clients are started on methadone, moved to Subutex, and then transitioned to Suboxone for maintenance. For those who desire eventual abstinence, gradual weaning from buprenorphine is much easier than from methadone. Another opioid substitute, levo-alpha acetylmethadol (LAAM), is still Food and Drug Administration (FDA)-approved, but the United States manufacturer ceased production in 2005. Both LAAM and methadone must be administered at limited-licensed clinics, while buprenorphine preparations can be prescribed at a doctor's office. This greatly reduces treatment burdens and has significantly benefitted clients.

18. C: The American Society of Addiction Medicine (ASAM) recognizes six interactive assessment dimensions: (1) acute intoxication or withdrawal potential (the level of intoxication or risk of severe withdrawal symptoms or seizures and exploring inpatient or ambulatory detoxification); (2) biomedical conditions and complications (other illnesses that may create risk or complicate treatment); (3) emotional, behavioral or cognitive conditions and complications (diagnosable mental disorders or mild, undiagnosable mental problems that complicate treatment); (4) readiness to change (open or resisting treatment, acknowledging or denying addiction, high or low motivations, etc.); (5) relapse, continued use or continued problem potential (immediate or low risk of substance use; good or poor coping or relapse prevention skills; severity of collateral problems such as suicidal behavior; etc.), and (6) recovery environment (influence or proximity of people, resources, and situations that may help or pose a threat to safety or continued treatment).

19. A: The most common distinguishing characteristic of a psychedelic drug is that users experience an alteration of their perception of reality. Psychedelic drugs are sometimes called hallucinogens because what users experience is similar to hallucinations.

20. B: Clinicians using the American Society of Addiction Medicine (ASAM) dimensions to guide treatment must first determine symptom severity. The first three dimensions of the ASAM include acute intoxication and/or withdrawal potential (Dimension 1), biomedical conditions and complications (Dimension 2), and emotional/behavioral or cognitive conditions/complications (Dimension 3). To operate within those dimensions, clinicians must have a working knowledge of pharmacology and symptoms of intoxication, overdose, and withdrawal. Determining symptom severity across the first three ASAM dimensions allows the client to receive immediate attention for severe medical impairment, noted in Dimension 1 and Dimension 2, and/or any emergent crisis (Dimension 3).

21. D: The Situational Confidence Questionnaire assesses a person's confidence in handling relapse triggers, including unpleasant emotions, loss of control, and physical unease. The Opioid Risk Tool – OUD can be used before a person is prescribed opioids for pain. It assesses an individual's level of risk by inquiring about mental conditions and any family and personal history of substance use (both legal and illegal). The Rosenberg Self-Esteem Scale uses a Likert scale to obtain global measures of self-worth. The Readiness to Change Questionnaire is based on the stages of change model used to assess a person's motivation to change substance use.

22. D: The overarching goal of behavioral health equity is to reduce persistent behavioral health disparities among affected populations. Behavioral health equity provides equal access to affordable, high-quality health services to help all individuals reach their highest potential. Behavioral health inequities persist in underserved populations characterized by specific geographical locations, gender, sexual orientation, age, race, disability, and income level. Multiple approaches are used to improve behavioral health disparities, including efforts to reduce medical mistrust, the use of high-quality evidence-based practices, and the provision of person-centered care.

23. C: Research shows that epigenetic factors account for 40–60% of a person's risk for addiction. Biological factors, including the interplay of genetics, environment, ethnicity, and gender, all influence a person's gene expression. Adolescents and individuals with mental disorders are at an increased risk for substance use disorder. Additional risk factors include poverty, peer and school stressors, early use, and family involvement with drugs and alcohol. Further, the more severe the manifestation of substance use, the more predominant the role of genetics. Theorists suggest a malfunction in neurotransmitter production results in a potentially profound need to self-medicate to compensate.

24. C: The diagnosis of alcohol use disorder (AUD) should be considered. The client admits to drinking four or five glasses of wine nightly and continues to use despite knowing the dangers of mixing alcohol with opiates (e.g., hydrocodone) and benzodiazepines (e.g., lorazepam). The client also exhibits withdrawal symptoms, as evidenced by drinking in the mornings to steady her nerves. She continues to place herself in risky situations by driving while intoxicated, and she is experiencing marital issues that are potentially related to her alcohol misuse. The client may misuse prescriptions, but substance misuse disorder is not a formal DSM-5-TR diagnosis. Although the client reports that her mother is diagnosed with bipolar disorder, there is insufficient information suggesting that the client meets the criteria for that diagnosis. She is more likely to meet the criteria for prolonged grief disorder. Substance-induced sleep disorders involve sleep difficulties caused by substances. The client endorses poor sleep, but there is insufficient information to determine if it is caused by substance use, depression, or an independent medical condition.

25. B: The counselor is not authorized to speak to the client's prescribers because the client did not sign an authorization to exchange confidential information. The client is mixing prescription medication with alcohol, placing her at higher risk for overdose; however, what is currently unknown is how often she uses the medications. The counselor has an ethical responsibility to inform the client of the risk, which the counselor accomplished and documented. The client admits to "fleeting" suicidal thoughts without a suicide plan and no prior attempts, which does not place her in immediate danger.

26. D: Alcohol impacts neurotransmitters by decreasing glutamate levels. When glutamate activity is inhibited by alcohol, alterations in mood, cognition, and memory occur. Alcohol increases dopamine (which activates the reward centers of the brain), serotonin (which affects emotion, attention, and motivation), and gamma-aminobutyric acid (which works to suppress the central nervous system) levels.

27. C: Intensive outpatient programs provide 9–20 hours of counseling per week and can last up to 12 weeks. Individuals in these programs receive individual, family, and group therapy and medication management. Brief therapy is an intervention or therapy rather than a modality. Outpatient therapy programs offer the same services as an intensive outpatient program with less frequency (e.g., weekly or biweekly). Residential treatment programs consist of around-the-clock live-in care and are staffed with full-time medical providers to assist residents with their daily needs.

28. A: The client is engaging in binge drinking. According to the Substance Abuse and Mental Health Services Administration, binge drinking for females involves four or more drinks in succession on the same occasion or within a couple of hours at least 1 day in the past month. Per the US Centers for Disease Control, for females, mild alcohol use or drinking in moderation is limiting drinks to one or less in a day and heavy alcohol use is defined as drinking eight drinks or more per week.

29. A: One of the case manager's roles is as an advocate for clients. The case manager can advocate for an individual client by informing other service providers about that client's specific needs. The case manager CAN also—and often must—educate other service providers not involved in treatment about the general characteristics of substance use and addiction, particularly if some providers are not knowledgeable in those areas. Case managers sometimes negotiate with agencies on their rules and regulations on behalf of a client to facilitate their ongoing involvement or the client's access. Moreover, when serving clients involved in the criminal justice system, case managers may need to advocate with the system to obtain sanctions that will facilitate the client's motivation and compliance with treatment.

30. B: Beneficence is the opposite of maleficence, and autonomy is the opposite of coercion. The core value of beneficence is to do good, or help others, whereas maleficence is to cause harm. Autonomy, another core ethical value, allows individuals to choose their direction in life; whereas coercion is to be controlled by another person. Competence involves having the requisite knowledge and skills to remain effective and current in clinical practice. Obedience is the responsibility that counselors have to observe and obey ethical and legal guidelines. Lastly, justice is the fair and ethical treatment of others.

31. C: The behavior component of BIRP progress recording is focused on counselor observations and client statements. It begins with subjective data (the client's observations, thoughts, and direct quotes) and moves to objective data (counselor observations of client affect, mood, appearance, etc.). The intervention section captures the counselor's efforts toward goals and objectives, general session content, whether homework was reviewed, and the goals and objectives addressed this session. Response refers to the client's intervention response and treatment plan goals and objectives progress. Plan involves documentation of what is to happen next, goals and objectives revisions, scheduled activities (sessions, group work, etc.), and any new or updated interventions.

32. D: Whether snorted, injected, or smoked, cocaine triggers the release of dopamine, serotonin, and norepinephrine. The primary effect occurs through the buildup of dopamine, though all neurotransmitters involved contribute to the subsequent euphoria. Not only does cocaine stimulate the release of these key neurotransmitters, but it also blocks their natural reabsorption by inhibiting a reuptake transporter from carrying out its normal functions. After the euphoria passes, neurotransmitter depletion induces a sense of profound dysphoria and depression, thus generating a need for further use of the drug. Individuals who are naturally deficient in serotonin appear to be particularly at risk for cocaine addiction.

33. C: When a drug is taken orally, it is dissolved within the stomach and then passes through the stomach lining or small intestine to enter the bloodstream.

34. B: Treatment planning should be a collaborative effort between the therapist and the client. The treatment plan should include the client's level of care during all phases of treatment. APs are ethically obligated to use ASAM or other relevant placement criteria to determine the client's level of care. Treatment plans must be updated at regular service intervals based on each client's individualized needs. Lastly, each goal, objective, intervention, and task must be individualized and incorporate components of the client's case conceptualization.

35. A: They ways that clients describe (or present) their symptoms may vary substantially across cultures. Asian clients, for example, are more likely to report somatic (physical) symptoms while omitting those of an emotional nature. Yet, when questioned specifically about emotional symptoms, these same clients will acknowledge them. Thus, clients from differing cultures may choose to selectively identify or omit symptoms in culturally acceptable ways. Cultures may also ascribe different meanings to an illness. These are typically derived from deep-seated attitudes and beliefs about whether an illness is real or imagined, arising from the body or the mind (or both), whether it may elicit sympathy, the potential degree of stigma attending it, potential causal factors, and a sense of the kind of person that might contract or succumb to it. These meanings ultimately determine whether or not a client feels motivated to seek treatment, ways they may cope with their symptoms, whether or not their family and community will be supportive, and from whom they seek help (doctor, counselor, religious leader or traditional healer, etc.).

36. B: Risk factors increase the likelihood of developing substance use disorders (SUDs), whereas protective factors reduce their impact. Protective factors cannot totally eliminate risk factors. For example, protective factors, such as self-esteem or academic competence, can mitigate risk factors for individuals genetically predisposed to SUD, but they do not completely eliminate them. Risk factors rarely occur in isolation but do exist in multiple contexts (e.g., community, family, individual). Risk factors can occur in specific groups (e.g., women, adolescents) or individuals (e.g., instances of prenatal exposure to substances). Lastly, risk factors are cumulative and co-occurring (e.g., parental SUD, child abuse, out-of-home placements).

37. B: Currently, this group comprises some 4 percent of the total US population and 25 percent of the total foreign-born population (nine of ten were born on foreign soil). Most of this heterogeneous group (more than half) live in only three states (California, Hawaii, and New York). Approximately 28 percent of Asian and Pacific Islanders report alcohol use, though only 3 percent report the use of illicit substances. This is the lowest rate of illicit substance abuse among all groups. Further, only 7 percent of adolescents in this group report alcohol use, as compared with 16 percent or more among whites, Hispanic or Latino, and Native American youth. However, it should be noted that there is great variation among various Asian and Pacific Islander groups. For example, illicit substance abuse rates by selected intragroup members are: Chinese (1 percent), Asian Indians (2 percent), Japanese (5 percent), and Koreans (7 percent). Consequently, careful assessments will be required.

38. B: An example of an amplified reflection is, "There are absolutely no consequences associated with your alcohol use." An amplified reflection evokes change talk by intensifying the client's sustain talk. This complex reflection is designed to be used sparingly. The response, "On the one hand, you would like to stop drinking, but on the other hand, you think it is not a problem for you" is a double-sided reflection. Double-sided reflections reflect both sides of the client's ambivalence to accentuate the discrepancy. The counselor stating, "You don't see a downside to your drinking, yet you just received a driving under the influence charge" is not a simple or complex reflection. With this statement, the spirit of motivational interviewing is not conveyed because the counselor is concluding that drinking is problematic based on a recent driving under the influence charge, rather than allowing the client to argue for change. Stating, "You really don't think alcohol is a problem for you" is a simple reflection.

39. C: The presence or absence of a substance or alcohol abuse problem is determined during the screening process, not during the evaluation and assessment process. During the evaluation and assessment, the presence of a problem is refined to reveal the nature of the problem, its diagnosis, and its extent and severity. Key goals and purposes of assessment include: (1) substance abuse history; (2) the severity and extent of the presenting substance or alcohol abuse problem; (3) co-occurring mental disorders; (4) legal issues that may contribute to or impede the treatment process (e.g., court-ordered treatment vs. detention or work-release issues, severe financial burdens of fines and court costs); (5) biomedical conditions and complications and stability for treatment; (6) available resources to help resolve the problem (family, social, employment-related, etc.); (7) client strengths, maturity, motivation, and readiness for treatment; and (8) the ideal treatment approach for optimal odds of success.

40. A: The acronym SIGECAPS is a tool prompting the full evaluation of the symptoms of depression. Each letter addresses one of the key potential features of depression: sleep (any significant increase or decrease), interests (decrease or loss of interest in previously pleasurable activities or events), guilt (feelings of guilt and burden without any real culpability or feelings that are disproportionate to actual circumstances), energy (decreased energy or feelings of listlessness, weariness or fatigue), concentration (decreased ability to focus and cognitively pursue thoughts in a meaningful way), appetite (increased or decreased appetite, as evidenced by weight loss or weight gain), psychomotor agitation or retardation (jittery tension and agitation or lethargy and sluggishness in movements), and suicidal ideation (persistent thoughts of self-harm, potentially escalating into increasingly detailed plans over time).

41. D: Individuals with substance use disorders run a much higher risk of suicidal thoughts and behaviors. Substances most likely to increase deaths by suicide are alcohol and opioids, with each of those substances double the rates of other illicit drugs. Research shows death rates as follows: opioids (22%), alcohol (20%), marijuana (10.2%), cocaine (4.6%), and amphetamines (3.4%) (Rizk et al, 2021). Individuals in treatment continue to run a substantially elevated risk of suicide; thus, treatment providers should be continuously aware of indicators of cascading risk (e.g., ideation, gestures, isolation, mood changes). The risk of suicide in treatment typically arises from factors concurrent with the decision to enter treatment: 1) they typically enter treatment when circumstances are out of control; 2) treatment is usually accepted in the face of multiple other life crises (job, marriage, health); and 3) seeking treatment often coincides with peak periods of concurrent depression.

42. C: Conditioned tolerance occurs when an unconditioned stimulus (i.e., psychoactive substance) is paired with conditioned stimuli (e.g., environmental cues). Cravings and triggers are caused by conditioned tolerance. The desire to use can be triggered by an emotion, smell, place, time of day, person, or location. Cross-tolerance occurs when tolerance to one substance results in tolerance to a pharmacologically similar substance (e.g., heroin and morphine). Reverse tolerance refers to increased sensitivity (i.e., sensitization) to a substance based on a person's changed neuronal activity. Individuals with reverse tolerance are generally long-term substance users who require smaller doses to achieve the desired effect. Dispositional tolerance occurs when an increase in a person's metabolism mitigates the effects of a substance, requiring higher doses to produce the desired effect.

43. B: According to the 2021 National Survey on Drug Use and Health (NSDUH), Hispanic populations were least likely to seek substance use disorder treatment. Estimates reported for individuals who received substance use disorder treatment in 2021 were: Asian (0.7%), Hispanic (1.0%), non-Hispanic whites (1.6%), and American Indian or Alaska Native (5.3%). Experts cite multiple causes of treatment disparities, including but not limited to heightened cultural stigma, racism, trauma, inequitable access to healthcare, socioeconomic difficulties, and inequitable services offered.

44. B: Gender-affirming care is an individualized treatment for LBGT youth with multiple components, excluding practices supporting conversion or reparative therapy. A wealth of empirical evidence indicates reparative therapy is medically inappropriate, nonbeneficial, and contraindicated. Gender-affirming care is designed to improve mental and physical health outcomes among LGBT youth experiencing gender dysphoria. Gender-affirming care includes developmentally appropriate psychoeducation regarding gender and sexuality, support of social transitioning, acknowledgment of intersectional identities, and garnering emotional support from families and communities for youth with variations in sexual orientation and gender identity. Lastly, gender-affirming care acknowledges that some, but certainly not all, youth will seek gender-affirming medical interventions.

45. B: The Substance Abuse and Mental Health Services Administration (SAMHSA) offers a Service Coordination Framework for Co-Occurring Disorders (i.e., Four Quadrants Model), which includes four categories based in symptom severity and the level of care required to meet client needs: Category I—mental disorders, less severe + substance use disorders, less severe; locus of care is a primary health care setting; Category II—mental disorders, more severe + substance use disorders, less severe; locus of care is a mental health system; Category III—mental disorders, less severe + substance use disorders, more severe; locus of care is a substance use treatment system; and Category IV—mental disorders, more severe + substance use disorders, more severe; locus of care includes but is not limited to state hospitals, jails or prisons, and emergency rooms.

46. C: Substance induced disorders involve psychiatric symptoms brought on by active substance use, intoxication, or withdrawal. There are 11 substance-induced disorders: 1) intoxication, 2) withdrawal, 3) delirium, 4) persisting dementia, 5) persisting amnesia, 6) psychosis, 7) mood disorders, 8) anxiety disorders, 9) sexual dysfunction, 10) sleep disorders, and 11) hallucination disorders. Clinicians must determine if the presenting disorder was substance induced or preexisting. Useful guidelines for a differential determination include: 1) secure a complete history (including collateral contacts, such as family, friends, etc.); 2) delay any determination for a month following the client's cessation of the substance; 3) evaluate the potential that the substance was used to self-medicate (ameliorate symptoms). The likelihood that the symptoms represent a preexisting condition occur in cases where symptoms persist longer than a month or were present before substance use.

47. B: LSD produces hallucinogenic effects when binding to serotonin 5-hydroxytryptamine 2A receptor (5-HT 2A) sites. Serotonin regulates body temperature, sleep, mood, digestion, and sensory perception. LSD also affects dopamine levels, which are responsible for coordination, pleasure, and motivation. Stimulants alter the synaptic levels of norepinephrine, dopamine, and serotonin. Alcohol, tranquilizers, opioids, and sedative-hypnotics have effects on the neurotransmitter GABA.

48. A: Microaggressions are damaging primarily because they are cumulative. Microaggressions are daily slights, derogatory comments, or insults that target individuals from marginalized groups. They originate from implicit bias, stereotypes, and prejudice and can be intentional or unintentional. When confronted, aggressors typically blame the person for being too sensitive or reading too much into subtle ambiguities, contributing to higher rates of mental and physical conditions among targeted individuals.

49. B: Opiates occur naturally and are derived from opium poppy plants. Opiates and are commonly used to manage pain. Examples of opioids include morphine, codeine, and heroin. Opiates differ from opioids in that opioids are produced synthetically, partially synthetically, or naturally.

50. A: According to the American Society of Addiction Medicine (ASAM) continuum of care, Level IV: Medically Managed Intensive Inpatient (i.e., withdrawal management in a hospital) is the highest level of care. The ASAM's general service continuum includes Level 1: Outpatient; Level II: Intensive Outpatient, Level III: Medically Monitored Intensive Inpatient, and Level IV: Medically Managed Intensive Inpatient. Withdrawal management in a residential setting corresponds with Level 3.7.

51. A: Many dual-diagnosed clients fare best in mutual-help groups specifically geared to those with co-occurring disorders. As all group members have co-occurring disorders, these so called double-trouble groups do a better job of accommodating psychiatric symptoms and supporting the use of necessary psychotropic medications. Double-trouble groups are not structured to offer formal counseling but instead allow members to support one another in achieving and maintaining recovery and holding each other accountable. Some of the more widely recognized groups include: (1) Double Trouble in Recovery; (2) Dual Disorders Anonymous; (3) Dual Recovery Anonymous; and (4) Dual Diagnosis Anonymous. Early research suggests that traditional twelve-step groups may be beneficial for clients with mild-to-moderate co-occurring psychiatric disorders. However, in cases of severe mental disorders, many clients may have difficulty attending traditional twelve-step groups. Some clients may choose to participate in both dual disorder and traditional mutual-help groups. Where they do, studies reveal that most Alcoholics Anonymous (AA) members respond positively, and as many 93 percent support the individual's adherence to his or her psychotropic medication regimen.

52. C: Both case management and client advocacy are subsets of service coordination, and resource linkage is one of the direct activities involved in each of these endeavors. Service coordination provides an action framework by which a client is enabled to achieve the specific goals identified in a treatment plan. It requires collaborative efforts not only between a case manager or counselor and a client but also with significant others as well as liaison activities with available agencies, service providers, managed care systems, and other community resources. Fundamental to service coordination is ongoing evaluation of client needs and treatment progress as well as resource referrals and advocacy as needed. The coordination and integration of treatment activities shared among various providers is a central feature of service coordination.

53. B: Clients requiring tertiary prevention programs for SUD would benefit most from outpatient treatment services. Preventative strategies exist along a continuum and include primary, secondary, and tertiary prevention. Primary prevention aims to prevent SUD before it occurs and includes community-wide education on its consequences. Secondary prevention involves screening to identify those at risk for SUD. In addition to screening, secondary prevention can include strategies for those in the early stages of SUD. Small group informational sessions to obtain SUD resources can be beneficial for these individuals. Lastly, tertiary prevention directs strategies toward individuals diagnosed with SUD. Tertiary prevention services exist on a continuum with tertiary interventions, including inpatient or outpatient services, mutual self-help support groups, and relapse-prevention strategies.

54. D: Drug cues include settings in which a drug was used, drug paraphernalia, and seeing others use drugs. Intense drug euphoria produces extremely intense, emotionally imprinted memory engrams, coupled with long-term changes in the amygdala area of the brain, which operate outside of conscious control. Key euphoric memories become integrally connected to sights, sounds, smells, people, and places previously associated with drug use. The reappearance of any of these past drug cues will often effectively trigger intense, amygdala-driven cravings for a drug. Cravings are further intensified by lingering imbalances in brain metabolism patterns, receptor availability, hormone levels, and other hypothalamus and pituitary-mediated sensations of dysphoria and distress. The cascading nature of these effects frequently induces a drug-use relapse.

55. B: In RPT, the therapist teaches cognitive-behavioral strategies to help clients manage cravings, recognize early warning signals, and reframe reactions to first lapses. In RPT assessment procedures, therapists help clients realize objectively the nature of their addiction; assess their motivation to change; and identify relapse risk factors. Therapists use techniques for raising awareness and insight to give clients alternative viewpoints (i.e., reframing lapses as a learning process rather than a moral failure) and help clients self-monitor for behavioral, emotional, and mental patterns related to substance use. Therapists also teach clients lifestyle modification strategies such as physical exercise, meditation, relaxation exercises.

56. A: Tolerance is the response to a drug that has developed when increased dosages are required over time to achieve the same effect as the original dose. When a person uses a drug over a long period, tolerance can develop, making it necessary for the dosage of the drug to be increased in order to achieve the same effects as the previous dosage. Dependence refers to the clinical or functional impairment resulting from continued use of a substance. Both tolerance and dependence result from the body and brain adapting to the repeated use of a substance. Withdrawal occurs when a substance upon which a person is dependent is abruptly discontinued, resulting in physiological symptoms. Toxicity occurs when a dose is received that has the potential for fatal or near-fatal events.

57. C: Early remission is no stimulant use criteria being met (except for craving) for at least 3 but less than 12 months. Sustained remission is no stimulant use criteria being met (except for cravings) for 12 months or longer. The terms full and partial are no longer used to describe remission.

58. C: The American Society of Addiction Medicine defines addiction as "a treatable, chronic medical disease involving complex interactions among brain circuits, genetics, the environment, and an individual's life experiences." This definition reinforces the notion that addiction is not solely a function of an individual's choice or a desired condition. Instead, addiction is viewed as a brain disease involving an intense compulsion to use substances despite adverse consequences.

59. A: Current trends in alcohol use among girls and young women ages 12–20 indicate higher instances of alcohol use than boys and young men ages 12–20. Compared to boys and young men, girls and women experience decreased societal acceptance surrounding alcohol use, are more likely to cope with mental disorders by drinking, and have higher BAC levels after consuming equal amounts of alcohol.

60. B: Rachel is diagnosed with major depressive disorder, which includes poor concentration as a diagnostic criterion. Feeling anxious and on edge is a symptom of generalized anxiety disorder. Argumentative behavior is commonly associated with oppositional defiant disorder, and risky alcohol use is a symptom of AUD.

61. D: Irregular breathing, measured by 10 or more seconds between breaths, is a symptom of alcohol toxicity. Slow breathing (fewer than eight breaths per minute) is also associated with alcohol toxicity. Hyposomnia, or a reduction in sleep, is associated with stimulant use. Alcohol use lowers body temperature, which can cause hypothermia rather than hyperthermia. Lastly, slurred speech is associated with alcohol intoxication and is less common with alcohol toxicity because the individual is generally nonresponsive.

62. C: Serious mental health issues, such as persistent suicidality, delusions, or hallucinations that precipitously resolve with abstinence are most likely substance abuse-induced disorders that will not reoccur without a return to the former substance abuse. In like manner, serious mental health issues that do not resolve in an abstinence period of thirty days or longer are likely due to an underlying mental disorder that must be evaluated and properly treated. In certain circumstances, an underlying mental disorder becomes exacerbated by substance abuse. In these situations, some measure of improvement will be noted, but it will fall substantially short of total resolution. This reflects the persistence of the underlying disorder; they will still need appropriate treatment for meaningful resolution of the condition.

63. D: According to *Painting the Current Picture: A National Report on Treatment Courts in the United States – Highlights & Insights* (Lanier et al., 2022), there has been a recent rise in stimulant use among participants in treatment court programs. Stimulant use was highest among family treatment court participants, followed by mental health court and adult drug court. In the general population (i.e., non-treatment court participants), reports of overdose deaths from methamphetamine use show a 7.5-fold increase between 2007 and 2017, with half of those deaths coupled with opioid use. The Midwest and West areas of the United States report significantly higher rates of methamphetamine use than the Northeast regions. Additionally, research findings indicate psychosocial interventions lead to improved outcomes for stimulant use disorder. These evidence-based practices include the Matrix model, cognitive-behavioral therapy, motivational interviewing, the community reinforcement approach, and contingency management.

64. A: This individual is the one most comprehensively responsible to evaluate, track, and coordinate the broad array of resources and services that a client is receiving in the treatment process. A service coordinator may assume some of these roles but is less involved in the clinical assessment and evaluation processes. A counselor or therapist may be very involved in clinical evaluations and assessments but would not typically be as involved in service coordination. Finally, an administrator looks after the management of a program or agency and thus would not typically be involved in frontline client evaluations and assessments or referrals and service coordination. Case management, however, addresses: assessment and evaluation (client capacity, progress and readiness, as well as agency, program, and resource availability and effectiveness), service coordination, referrals and referral network management, monitoring, tracking, problem solving, advocating, negotiating, offering liaison services, and arranging and carrying out the resource needs of a treatment plan.

65. C: Alcohol is the most commonly used central nervous system depressant. According to the National Institute of Health (NIH), In the past year, individuals over the age of 12 have used alcohol more than any other substance, and the most common substance disorder is alcohol use disorder. Alcohol, in all its forms, slows down the body's processes and is therefore known as a depressant. It is commonly used in one of three forms: beer, wine, or distilled spirits. One of the reasons for its widespread use is that it is legally obtainable.

66. D: The most common symptom of Wernicke's encephalopathy is confusion. Other symptoms include poor muscle coordination and oculomotor impairment (problems moving the eyes in a controlled fashion). Wernicke's syndrome is a short-term condition resulting from vitamin B1 (thiamine) deficiency, typically developing after years of drinking and poor nutrition. Of those with Wernicke's syndrome, 80–90% will develop long-term psychosis and memory problems known as Korsakoff syndrome. While poor coordination is a symptom, retrograde amnesia (loss of old memories) and learning impairments are among the more classic hallmarks of the condition. Because they are so often found together, the two syndromes are often referred to concurrently as Wernicke-Korsakoff syndrome.

67. D: Counselors working with substance abusers are often exposed to traumatic narratives from clients with extensive histories of abuse (especially parent to child) and life chaos. When unrelieved, these narratives can accumulate and lead to posttraumatic stress disorder (PTSD)-like symptoms in counselors—difficulty concentrating, diminished affect, irritability, troubling dreams, compromised sleep, intrusive thoughts, free-floating anxiety, and so on. Accompanying feelings of anger, fear, or helplessness are common.

The result can be counselor numbness and detachment, unconsciously dismissing client feelings and traumas, or overinvestment with parent-like caregiving or even inappropriate efforts at problem solving, rescuing, and failing to guide the client to essential growth. In these situations, counselors must seek supportive supervision and guidance to overcome emotional burdens and problematic responses.

68. D: Reforming current drug laws is vital to mitigating treatment inequities in communities of color because current laws have perpetuated generational trauma and inequitable access to treatment in these communities. Current laws do not reflect the concept that SUD is a treatable medical disease but rather a punishable condition and moral failure. America's war on drugs initiative has been costly, ineffective, and has reinforced stereotypes among black and Hispanic populations. Individuals in communities of color, particularly men, are disproportionately punished for nonviolent drug offences than their white counterparts. Principle III-29 of the NAADAC Code of Ethics (2021) addresses the importance of advocacy efforts and the need for APs to become aware of the stigma and prejudice toward people with SUD.

69. A: In becoming ready to seek change and overcome past habits and addictions, clients typically go through five stages of change: (1) pre-contemplation, (2) contemplation, (3) action, (4) relapse, and (5) maintenance. By virtue of having entered treatment, the client is already at the action stage in the readiness process. Consequently, when client resistance to treatment is encountered, this resistance most likely indicates that the client has been pressured to move too quickly through the change process, leaving him or her little opportunity to respond with anything but resistance. Exploring the client's current rationale and determination to change can reveal where he or she is on the change continuum, enabling the counselor to better support the client along the way.

70. A: The primary function of a release of information is to allow the counselor to communicate confidential information to a specified party. The release of information must be signed and identify which information is requested, including but not limited to client diagnosis, assessment information, recommendations, school reports, and psychiatric evaluation. A release of information must also specify a person intended to receive or produce client information, such as a teacher, family member, or outside professional. A release of information does not give the counselor a blanket right to provide or receive information whenever they deem appropriate. Additionally, a subpoena is required to release court records, and HIPAA protects identifiable information from being released without client consent.

71. A: The original twelve-step program, Alcoholics Anonymous (AA) had a significant religious orientation. Since that time, however, references to deity and religion in general have been moderated to better allow for individual values and beliefs. A group similar to AA but oriented toward those using narcotics is known as Narcotics Anonymous (NA). Some clients may also benefit from twelve-step support group alternatives such as Rational Recovery, Smart Recovery, or Women for Sobriety. Offering clients a variety of choices empowers them to make informed decisions. There are also twelve-step meetings designed to support the family members of loved ones suffering from substance abuse. These include: Al-Anon/Alateen and Nar-Anon. Other twelve-step groups exist for individuals coping with compulsive behaviors such as sex, gambling, spending, and eating. Helping clients and their family members to find and join appropriate mutual-help organizations can be an important part of treatment planning and continuing care.

72. A: Housing First is an evidence-based approach to housing insecurity grounded in the principle of consumer choice. Individuals who experience housing insecurity cannot afford housing because of a financial setback, job loss, physical or psychological disability, or substance use disorder. There are no prerequisites (e.g., sobriety, motivation to change) for accessing supportive services through Housing First. Research indicates that consumers are more likely to access supportive services when they have the freedom to choose these services. Housing First principles also include immediate access to housing, community engagement, individual wellbeing, and needs-based treatment. Harm-reduction strategies are emphasized but not required, which differs from the principle of nonmaleficence (i.e., "to do no harm"), as the latter is a counseling principle applied in the context of a therapeutic relationship.

73. B: Asking the client for permission to discuss the subject of change is a good way to display your respect for the autonomy of the client, which in turn encourages the client to trust you. Client expectations, such as the duration of the session, the goals for treatment, and how future sessions will be conducted are necessary components of informed consent. These items help structure or frame treatment. Asking the client for permission to discuss change helps form the basis of the therapeutic alliance and allows other issues to organically transpire instead of the counselor informing or telling the client what will happen.

74. A: Addiction causes neuroadaptation, which stimulates a craving, or a strong urge to obtain and consume a substance when it is absent or discontinued. A craving occurs when a person seeks to reexperience the dopamine surge created by active addiction. Relapse occurs when a person resumes substance use after a period of abstinence. Tolerance also results from neuroadaptation, forcing the brain to accommodate higher volumes of a substance, requiring higher doses to achieve the effects previously obtained with lower doses. Withdrawal occurs after a chronically used addictive substance is abruptly discontinued, setting a cascade of physical, emotional, and cognitive reactions in motion.

75. B: The quickest and most intense route of administration is intravenous. The effects of substances administered intravenously can be experienced within 30 and 60 seconds. IV injections are immediately introduced into the circulatory system, making overdoses more common as higher quantities can be administered quickly. The effects from medications ingested or administered orally often occur within 30-90 minutes, while drugs that are snorted or administered nasally can be experienced in 5-10 minutes. Lastly, many substances that are absorbed rectally take effect in 5-30 minutes.

76. A: Compared to adults of all ages, rates of illicit drug use among older adults are steadily increasing, while rates of co-occurring mental disorders are also high. For this reason, a comprehensive assessment is recommended to determine the presence of substance misuse and differentiate this diagnosis from co-occurring mental disorders and other age-related symptoms (e.g., cognitive functions). Older adults are particularly at risk for developing an opioid use disorder due to higher instances of chronic pain. Older adults metabolize drugs at slower rates and often take multiple prescription medications. According to the 2019 National Survey on Drug Use and Health (NSDUH), 37% of older adults diagnosed with substance use disorder also had a mental disorder

77. D: The Diagnostic Interview Schedule (DIS) provides diagnostic information about alcohol and other substance-use disorders as well as anxiety disorders, depression, eating disorders, schizophrenia, and antisocial personality disorder, among other psychiatric conditions. The instrument explores syndromes meeting DSM criteria over the past year along with information about the course of the disorders, functional impairments, and any perceived need for treatment, treatment utilization, and potential links between psychiatric and physical symptoms. It also establishes dates for more recent symptoms and risk factors. Primary concerns are that it requires more than the 90–120 estimated minutes to administer (averaging 2.5 hours, per one study), and that it fails to consistently identify clients with depression or schizophrenia. However, the highly structured content and administration guidelines do allow trained non-clinicians to administer it accurately.

78. B: Gambling disorder has an established DSM-5-TR diagnostic criteria identifying it as a mental disorder. Criteria for this disorder specify that gambling must lead to clinically significant impairment or distress in 12 months. Additionally, four or more (out of nine) symptoms must be met; specifications for episodic or early remission and current severity are also assigned. Although other process addictions are included in the DSM-5-TR as conditions warranting additional consideration, gambling disorder is the only process addiction classified as a mental disorder. To qualify as an SUD, caffeine use disorder requires further study to determine the correlates of the proposed criteria, prevalence, and clinical significance.

79. B: Confirmation bias involves selectively organizing information to match or validate preexisting beliefs and ideas. Affinity bias refers to the tendency to be drawn toward individuals who are most like ourselves. Conformity bias (i.e., groupthink) occurs when individuals in group settings change their viewpoints or match those expressed by the group. Attribution bias involves the tendency for a person to attribute successes to one's abilities and failures to external circumstances.

80. A: The strengths that combine to produce resiliency include: (1) insight (asking essential questions, accepting honest answers, and thereby developing a mature understanding of self, others, and situations); (2) independence (balancing proper personal boundaries against the need for family bonds and affection and separating from the family if needed); (3) wholesome relationships (finding substitute parents or mentors, as needed, with balanced attachments); (4) initiative (able to accomplish goals and tasks from which is drawn proper self-esteem and a pleasure in achievement that promotes ongoing growth and development); (5) creativity or humor (imaginative creativity to make nothing into something positive); (6) humor (the ability to laugh at oneself and circumstances so as to turn something negative into nothing); and (7) morality (a well-informed conscience that serves and alleviates suffering in others). Fostering these strengths in children, youth, and adults can help them develop into highly resilient individuals.

81. C: The five main levels in the substance abuse continuum of care, as identified by the American Society of Addiction Medicine (ASAM) are: Level 0.5: early intervention services (subclinical or pretreatment, exploring risks and addressing problems or risk factors that appear to be related to substance use); Level I: outpatient services (nonresidential, less than nine hours per week); Level II: intensive outpatient or partial hospitalization services— nonresidential, a minimum of nine hours per week (Level II is subdivided into levels II.1 and II.5); Level III: residential or inpatient services—minimum of twenty-five hours per week (Level III is subdivided into levels III.1, III.3, III.5, and III.7); and Level IV: medically managed intensive inpatient services (subacute, with daily physician supervision). These levels are not discrete but rather points on a treatment continuum.

82. A: GATE was established by a consensus panel addressing the evaluation of suicidal ideation and behaviors by substance abuse counselors working with at-risk clients. GATE is an acronym that stands for: Gather information, Access supervision, Take responsible action, and Extend the action. Gathering information involves (1) screening for suicidality and (2) observing for warning signs. Screening involves direct questions regarding current thoughts (plans, means, or preparations) and any past history of attempts. Accessing supervision or consultation (even if the counselor already has specialized training) ensures issues of risk are fully evaluated. Taking responsible action protects client well-being and safety. Extending the action involves securing follow-up and ongoing monitoring as needed. In this way, GATE fully assesses and addresses suicidality. The final step is thorough documentation to secure a medical and legal record of the care provided.

83. B: Empathy is the ability to understand what another person is experiencing. Empathy does not involve feeling what the client is feeling but instead having the ability to understand those feelings and communicate that back to the client. Sympathy is often associated with feeling pity for another person, whereas empathy is a deeper expression of compassion and understanding. Counselors show empathy by metaphorically placing themselves in their clients' shoes—reflecting an understanding of their perceptions, feelings, and worldviews.

84. C: Addiction is a chronic, treatable, and preventable disease that causes significant impairment in functioning, with long-term but reversible changes in brain chemistry. Treatment for SUD and behavioral addictions requires ongoing monitoring and support to sustain recovery.

85. D: Cocaine does the most damage to the heart. Considerable medical research demonstrates that cocaine not only causes arterial constriction secondary to the drug's stimulant effects, but it also causes a cumulative effect, with more cocaine causing increased arterial narrowing.

Atherosclerosis (artery hardening and plaque buildup) greatly magnifies this deleterious process. The result is that permanent disability or death due to sudden cardiac arrest or hemorrhagic cerebral stroke is an increasingly real possibility the longer the drug is abused. Finally, cocaine-induced damage to the prefrontal lobes (where behaviors are modified and controlled) often results in impaired judgment, disinhibition, loss of foresight, decisional incapacity, and chronic unpredictability and irritability.

86. D: Participation in twelve-step and other mutual-help programs is associated with better outcomes than participation in treatment programs alone. Indeed, clients who join a twelve-step program after treatment tend to do significantly better than those not so involved, researchers have found. Consequently, treatment providers should facilitate client integration into appropriate community-based mutual-help groups, including assisting clients to locate a group and a sponsor. This should involve more than referral. Counselors should help clients find the right group meeting milieu as well as helping them determine the optimal frequency of attendance. Clients who begin attending twelve-step groups frequently experience some minor negative side effects. These can be minimized by ensuring selection of an optimal group, along with adequate orientation and support.

87. B: APs ensure clients' records are securely stored, maintained, and protected against unauthorized persons during the process of acquiring informed consent. Principle II-2 of the NAADAC Code of Ethics (2021) outlines informed consent to include any treatment information, limitations to confidentiality, and any risks, benefits, and limitations associated with treatment. Clients must be informed of their rights and responsibilities verbally and in writing. Duty to warn is a breach of confidentiality that occurs when the counselor must warn third parties at risk of client harm. While a review of client rights, including record storage, may occur during an initial intake interview, informed consent is a signed document indicating that the client understands the client's and counselor's rights and responsibilities.

88. D: The higher power concept arises from twelve-step programs themselves. Cognitive-behavioral therapy (CBT) posits emotional and behavioral reactions are largely learned responses and that alternative responses can be learned. Thus, the CBT approach teaches clients how to recognize and limit relapse risks, behaviors to maintain abstinence, and techniques to improve self-efficacy while identifying cues or triggers (feelings, situations, and people) that may promote substance use. Triggers are either internal (e.g., stress responses, cravings, etc.) or external (e.g., people, places, or situations in which drugs were used). By analyzing triggers, adopting new recovery-oriented responses, and role-playing high-risk scenarios, clients develop the skills to resist substance use urges. CBT approaches also work well for other recovery challenges (e.g., relationships, mood management, etc.). CBT and twelve-step approaches complement each other well. Thus, many CBT-oriented programs encourage twelve-step program participation.

89. D: Psychoeducational groups teach key concepts regarding substance use disorder and its consequences. These time-limited groups are ideal for education at the outset of treatment. Their educational nature permits an objective examination of dysfunctional beliefs, problem thinking patterns, along with relapse prevention and skills training. Skills-development groups focus on refusal training, relapse prevention, assertiveness training, and stress management. Support groups, such as 12-step programs, help members maintain sobriety, examine conditions leading to substance misuse, determine associated consequences, and make amends for any wrongdoing. Interpersonal process groups include single-interest groups (focused on specialized issues, usually later in treatment) and family or couples groups that explore the effects of substance use on relationships.

90. B: The three components of Maslach and Jackson's multidimensional theory of burnout are emotional exhaustion, depersonalization, and reduced professional efficacy. Lee experiences emotional exhaustion, which is evidenced by coming to work late, missing work, exhaustion, and feeling physically sick when arriving to work. His supervisory meeting reveals that Lee also experiences reduced professional efficacy, and he is noted to experience depersonalization when eventually becoming apathetic and detached from clients. Vicarious trauma occurs with repeated exposure to trauma. Lee experiences a lack of professional support, which contributes to his burnout but is not one of the three components of the theory of burnout. For Lee, overidentification with clients results in poor boundaries and countertransference, which are not essential components of burnout.

91. C: Lee's reaction to Marcus is an example of countertransference. Countertransference occurs when a counselor's unconscious thoughts and feelings are redirected onto a client. Lee's resurfaced feelings of inferiority were triggered by his supervisor placing him on a performance improvement plan, which he believed was unfair. These feelings were then projected onto Marcus, who Lee feels has had no repercussions for his actions and who has a family who cares. Transference is when clients project their unconscious thoughts and feelings onto the counselor. Triangulation occurs when a third party enters a dyadic relationship to provide distance or stability. Counselors experience secondary traumatization when repeated exposure to a client's or multiple clients' traumatic material causes symptoms similar to those who experienced it firsthand.

92. C: Lee's interaction with Jada is most likely an example of a boundary violation. Boundary violations occur when a counselor is in a dual (i.e., personal and professional) relationship with a client that is harmful, deceitful, exploitative, or manipulative. Lee is in a position of authority as an adult and as Jada's therapist. He accepts a hug from Jada and promises to keep her sexual relationship a secret. This is an abuse of power and could potentially stem from Lee's unmet needs and feelings of inadequacy.

93. B: Lee's actions are most likely unethical. Principle II-3 of the NAADAC Code of Ethics (2021) states that APs "shall limit access of the client to their records, and provide a summary of the records when there is evidence that full access could cause harm to the client." It is unclear whether the discovery of Jada's sexual relationship would send Jada back to her father or whether Jada's statement about her abusive father is substantiated. Lee does have an ethical responsibility to ensure that Jada is adequately supervised at both residences. Lee is also responsible for documenting the conversation and engaging in ethical decision-making to determine if he should disclose the relationship. Principle II-17 of the code states that APs must protect the confidentiality of minor clients who cannot provide voluntary informed consent. However, research suggests that individuals ages 14–15 have the cognitive capacity to make adult decisions and should be offered the same confidentiality protections as adults (Brooks et al., 2013). There are also ethical and legal limitations to confidentiality (see Principle II-7 of the code). Lee's performance improvement plan addresses administrative expectations. Scope of practice refers to the legal and ethical activities that an AP can engage in as a result of requisite knowledge, skills, training, and experience. Each state defines the scope of practice for credentialed professionals. Because Lee is a certified AP, he is within his scope of practice.

94. B: Cocaine has a short half-life with nearly half of the cocaine absorbed into the body being excreted in urine within 1 hour. The effects of smoking methamphetamine can last between 8 and 12 hours, whereas the euphoria from smoking crack cocaine lasts up to 20 minutes. Smoking crack cocaine results in a more intense high than snorting cocaine. Acute withdrawal rather than intoxication is characterized by dysphoria, agitation, and anxiety.

95. A: The Alcohol Use Disorders Identification Test is a three-item instrument used to assess the frequency and quantity of alcohol use, with points given for the severity of each affirmative answer. For example, question 1 asks "How often did you have a drink containing alcohol in the past year?" The respondent receives 0 points for never, 1 point for monthly or less, 2 points for two to four times a month, 3 points for two to three times a week, and 4 points for four or more times a week. Question 2 asks "How many drinks did you have on a typical day when you were drinking in the past year?" Question 3 asks "How often did you have six or more drinks on one occasion in the past year? The Global Appraisal of Individual Needs is used to identify individuals with behavioral health disorders for whom a full 1.5- to 2-hour assessment would be useful. The Drug Abuse Screening Test-1 is a one-item inventory that asks "In the last 12 months, have you used drugs other than those required for medical reasons?" with affirmative responses warranting the use of the Drug Abuse Screening Test-10. The Brief Screener for Tobacco, Alcohol, and Other Drugs includes frequency-of-use questions to assist clinicians in identifying risky substance use among adolescents.

96. D: The Suicide Behaviors Questionnaire-Revised is a four-item instrument. It assesses suicidal ideation in a person's recent past (i.e., within the past 12 months), present, or lifetime and the likelihood of suicidal acts in the future. The Columbia–Suicide Severity Rating Scale contains a series of questions used to assess the severity of suicidality and determine the level of support required. It asks about suicidal ideation, actions taken to prepare for suicide and in what timeframe, whether there has been a previous attempt, and whether any attempt was thwarted by another person or by the client. The DSM-5 Self-Rated Level 1 Cross-Cutting Symptom Measure is a 23-item questionnaire that assesses 13 psychiatric domains occurring within the previous 2 weeks. The Mental Health Screening Form-III is a 17-item questionnaire used to assess co-occurring mental disorders.

97. C: Women currently account for 23% of human immunodeficiency virus (HIV) cases in the US. While overall cases have dropped 24% from 2010, there still remains concern over missed opportunities for prevention and intervention. Data from 2018 indicate that Black females accounted for 58% of all HIV case among women, while only accounting for just over 10% of the female population. Individuals at risk for HIV include those residing in communities with high transmission rates, substance use, impulsivity and other high-risk activities, and individuals experiencing intimate partner violence. Men engaging in unprotected anal sex with other men are most affected by HIV. Females engaging in unprotected sex with men diagnosed with HIV have higher rates of contraction than males engaging in unprotected sex with women diagnosed with HIV.

98. B: The potential client should not feel that it is required for him or her to seek treatment elsewhere, though he or she may choose to do so. Regardless, it is important for the counselor and the potential client to address any immediate concerns. This is usually handled best by way of a brief, private conversation between the two—perhaps in the privacy of the counselor's office. There, the existence of a prior social relationship can be acknowledged, and the potential client can be assured that the counselor will not involve him- or herself in the client's treatment in any way. Further, standards of confidentiality can also be explained, and the acquaintance can also be assured that he or she is fully in control of how to deal with this shared knowledge outside the treatment setting. To ensure the client's comfort and confidentiality as fully as possible, he or she must also disclose the acquaintance to supervising staff. In this way, the counselor can ensure that he or she will not ever be involved in the client's treatment in any way.

99. B: The primary reason that ordered and routine activities are built into the therapeutic community (TC) treatment process is to establish consistency and predictability. Once clients experience consistency and predictability, their lives become less complicated, and they can build self-reliance and a positive work ethic. Successful attainment of skills may be reinforced by earning community privileges or attaining a lower level of care. Still, the primary reason is for clients to begin to rebuild their lives around rehabilitation and recovery. TC treatment protocols consist of phases and stages that allow tracking client activities and measuring progress. Treatment duration is dependent upon successful client progress. Staff and peer networks offer support, and other community-based services are integrated as needed to sustain recovery. The TC treatment approach is ideal for clients with past criminal issues, educational and employment deficits, relationship problems, and a history of failed treatment. A drug-free environment must be ensured when used in an intensive outpatient program.

100. C: A functional analysis examines a person's triggers and consequences associated with substance use. Functional analyses are performed to identify the need for treatment or to individualize relapse prevention plans. The analysis includes all activities, places, and people influencing use. Other functional factors include emotions and psychological pathways that maintain or predispose a person to substance use. The analysis extends to all negative consequences, including family, health, finances, marriage, employment, and legal and social outcomes. Additional assessment inquiries include questions related to quantity consumed (including proof or purity), frequency of use, types of substances, and whether a person is engaging in polysubstance use. A physiological assessment focuses on blood, breath, and urine tests. Functional tolerance refers to a person's lessened response to a substance. Physical and physiological dependencies rely upon a person's threshold for feeling functionally "normal" (i.e., the quantity of alcohol required to avoid withdrawal). Lastly, looking into a person's behaviors that interfere with one's basic needs is a principle associated with reality therapy.

101. B: The earliest Matrix Model was developed as a twelve-month version that included six months of intensive treatment with fifty-six individual or family counseling sessions. Counseling was provided three or four times each week, augmented with educational, family, relapse prevention, and social support groups. The first cocaine-specific treatment protocol was eventually revised to address alcohol and opioid use as well. Ultimately, cost constraints led to the development of a sixteen-week model that reduced individual sessions to three and focused more on group work. The individual program eventually expanded to include a twelve-week family and patient education group series and continuing care via an ongoing weekly social support group for continuing care. The program is rounded out with weekly drug testing (urinalysis) and encouragement to attend twelve-step meetings to supplement the intensive treatment and provide a continuing source of positive emotional and social support.

102. C: Screening is a process of examining a client for one or more specific potential problems, while assessment defines the nature and extent of the problem and offers treatment recommendations. Assessment involves a clinical evaluation of client functioning and generally uses multiple sources to drawn to inferences about specific aspects of a person. A basic assessment includes fundamental information gathering and examination of client problems, strengths, disabilities, co-occurring disorders, and readiness for change. Once formalized, relevant aspects of CODs are integrated into the treatment plan formulation and application.

103. A: Open-ended heterogeneous groups allow clinicians some flexibility in assigning new clients to ongoing groups. This permits immediate responsiveness to new and early client needs. However, those in these open-ended heterogeneous groups vary in their recognition and acceptance of their substance abuse. Thus, over time, it usually becomes necessary to move clients into progress- or issue-specific groups as unique needs and progress become apparent. Some clients make rapid progress from one stage to another, while others may need to return to an earlier treatment stage due to relapse or encountering other problems. In this way, the treatment process can be meaningfully individualized and tailored to the unique and changing needs of each client. Because of this, the group to which a given client was initially assigned is unlikely to remain unchanged throughout the treatment episode.

104. D: The acronym DIG-FAST is a tool prompting the full evaluation of manic symptoms. Each letter addresses one of the key potential features of mania: distractibility, as evidenced by an inability to concentrate; indiscretion or reckless behaviors (e.g., substance misuse, sexual indiscretions); grandiosity, as evidenced by larger-than-life feelings of superiority, wealth, or power; flight of ideas, which involves racing thoughts and incoherent speech.; activity, which can manifest as increased psychomotor activity or restlessness; sleep deficit; and talkativeness as evidenced by pressured speech.

105. D: Properly written progress notes chart client progress toward the goals, objectives, and action steps included on the treatment plan. Progress notes are used to explain and inform any changes to the treatment plan by recording what transpires during each clinical interaction. Progress notes can be used to document client experiences, behaviors, level of functioning, motivation, and response to intervention. In this respect, progress notes are a snapshot in time reflecting each client's current status in a chronological, objective, comprehensive, non-biased, and factual manner. Progress toward the treatment plan goals is recorded, with regular treatment plan updates remaining consistent with the changes documented on client progress notes

106. B: Just under 2/3 of cannabis is excreted in a person's feces. Marijuana is absorbed through the bloodstream and produces a short peak effect (longer if taken orally rather than smoked). It is metabolized and eliminated mostly through the user's feces, and 20% is excreted through the urine.

107. C: The concept of nonmaleficence is an ethical principle drawn from the biomedical literature. It refers to the ancient medical tenant *Primum Non Nocere* (Latin: first, do no harm—i.e., never make a problem worse). Medication-assisted treatment of opioid addiction has been challenged as enlarging or at least perpetuating an addictive problem. However, given the serious risks of illicit opioid use, ethicists have dismissed these concerns.

Other key ethical principles are: (2) beneficence—working for the benefit and well-being of all clients (e.g., proper diagnosis, evidence-based treatments); (3) autonomy—often referred to as self-determination, this principle emphasizes respect for client rights to make well-informed choices that meet their own desires and life goals (it assumes a client has been fully informed of all risks and benefits of available options, and properly understands them); (4) justice—requires treatment providers to act fairly, equally, and equitably, especially when resources are limited; and (5) fidelity—faithfulness in honoring commitments and obligations (not abandoning clients, making and supporting proper referrals, etc.).

108. B: Integrated behavioral health care is associated with reducing societal stigma for individuals seeking treatment for opioid use disorder (OUD). The stigma associated with SUD is reflected in negative societal attitudes and stereotypes. This is particularly true for individuals with OUD. The recommended treatment for OUD combines medication-assisted treatment with behavioral and psychological interventions. Integrated behavioral health care is critical for managing withdrawal symptoms and providing medication-assisted treatment, thereby moving from stand-alone care for addiction to an approach that reinforces the notion that addiction is a treatable disease, much like diabetes and other medical conditions.

109. B: Telescoping is a phenomenon used to describe substance use disparities according to gender. Despite late initiation to substance use, women accelerate their consumption rates more quickly than men. As a result, women tend to enter treatment for SUDs with more advanced physical, social, emotional, and behavioral difficulties. Substance use disparities exist among age groups, race and ethnicity, and sexual orientation; however, telescoping specifically refers to gender disparities.

110. C: Substance abuse issues may develop at any time throughout the life course; however, the most significant risk is adolescence. This group is particularly vulnerable for numerous reasons, including (1) the developing brain is more susceptible to the changes induced by substance use; (2) the likelihood of exposure to substances increases at this time; (3) peer pressure and the increased social demands of dating and relationships; (4) an increased likelihood for engaging in risk-taking; (5) hormonal and other developmental changes inducing further instability.

111. B: Principle III-39 of the NAADAC Code of Ethics (2021) states that APs shall not refer clients from their places of employment to their private practice without prior documented authorization. APs must also provide multiple referral options to clients in need. Additionally, supervision and consultation should be obtained to address potential or actual conflicts of interest and recommendations must be documented.

112. C: The Outcome Rating Scale, along with the Session Rating Scale, is part of the Partners for Change Outcomes Management System used to measure treatment progress and the therapeutic alliance, respectively. The Outcome Rating Scale is administered at the beginning of each therapy session and is reviewed in session with the therapist to course-correct treatment interventions or adjust strategies to reinforce the progress already made. The Health of the Nation Outcome Scales is a 12-scale therapist-rated instrument used to guide treatment and measure client change. The Outcome Questionnaire is a more extensive 45-item assessment measuring symptom distress, interpersonal relations, and social roles throughout treatment and after discharge; it also screens for suicidal ideation, anger and violence, and substance use in various settings. The Daily Living Activities measures a client's level of functioning encompassing 20 activities of daily living across 10 domains (e.g., health practices, communication, time management, and drug and alcohol use).

113. D: Marijuana affects each person differently. Depending on the strain or the amount used, marijuana can produce depressant effects (e.g., drowsiness, relaxation, dizziness), stimulant effects (e.g., elevated mood, rapid heart rate, anxiety), or cause the user to experience hallucinations. MDMA (aka ecstasy [pill form] or Molly [crystal form])acts as a hallucinogen and stimulant. LSD and ketamine are both hallucinogens.

114. C: The Health Insurance Portability and Accountability Act of 1986 Privacy Rule offers federal protections for covered entities allowing client access to their personal health information with the exception of psychotherapy notes. Psychotherapy notes are private notes kept by the client's provider and are not part of the clinical record. They are often used to document clinical impressions, examine a hypothesis, or document points regarding follow-up care. Case notes (i.e., patient encounters), on the other hand, are part of the client's medical record and do not have the same protection as psychotherapy notes.

115. C: HIV cannot be transmitted through coughing or sneezing. HIV is commonly transmitted via blood, semen, breast milk, vaginal fluids, and anal mucus. While HIV cannot be cured, it can be treated with antiretroviral therapy (ART). Populations at greater risk for HIV include individuals engaging in high-risk behaviors, including anal sex and needle sharing. Individuals with substance use disorder are at higher risk of HIV due to heightened impulsivity, disinhibition, and failure to use appropriate precautions when engaging in intravenous drug use and sexual activity. Among the general population, adolescents and young adults are at higher risk for HIV infection.

116. A: This size facilitates optimal treatment engagement without permitting individual neglect. Process-oriented groups may be more effective with only six to eight members as these middle- to late-phase groups focus more on daily issues, thoughts, emotions, behavior management, and new ways of relating to others. Psychoeducational groups can be larger as they primarily involve didactic content. Many group sessions are structured using a rule of thirds. The first third involves sharing current issues or experiences; the second third addresses a particular issue or skill; and, the final third is used to summarize learnings and assign an exercise. An alternative structure involves a problem-solving process: (1) an issue of concern is identified; (2) options and solutions are explored; (3) an optimal course is identified; and (4) an action plan is developed. This is followed by soliciting commitments from group members to attempt the solution and report the outcome. Finally, many recovery groups utilize opening and closing rituals that enhance commitments and group solidarity.

117. C: The Treatment Services Review (TSR) is designed for use in conjunction with the Addiction Severity Index (ASI). The TSR is a ten-minute structured interview that assesses the nature and frequency of treatment services provided for a client in the following domains: (1) medical problems; (2) substance use (alcohol and drug) problems; (3) employment and support problems; (4) family problems; (5) legal problems; and (6) psychological or emotional problems. Each domain is comprised of three sections. The first section reports the number of days that a target behavior or problem occurred. The second section records the number of times (per week) that a professional has provided services. The third section captures the number of structured sessions that were held for a particular problem during the prior week—whether through the index treatment program (in-program) or by others (out-program). The TSR provides a continuous record of the number and types of services provided, the rate at which these identified problems show change, and measures cost-effectiveness among the patient population that actually receives the services.

118. A: Cheryl's best course of action would be to decline the role and provide information on alternatives. APs must make every effort to avoid dual relationships with clients. Debra resides in a rural community; however, she receives e-therapy, which provides her with the technology necessary to access online 12-step meetings and mutual support groups.

119. C: Constructing a medically necessary treatment plan begins with a thorough biopsychosocial assessment. Treatment plans serve as a roadmap for treatment. Ethically sound treatment plans are client-directed and therapist driven. Debra presents with multiple treatment issues, including attention deficit hyperactivity disorder (ADHD), reunification with her children, reintegration into the community, sobriety, anxiety, and poor concentration. A biopsychosocial assessment will help narrow the treatment focus, provide structure, ensure that the client receives appropriate treatment, and determine if outside referrals are necessary. Once the assessment is complete, Cheryl and Debra can then identify and prioritize treatment issues and unresolved problems. Cheryl is an AP, making consultation from a child abuse specialist less likely to contribute to a medically necessary treatment plan. However, reunification issues are likely to require a referral to a specialized therapist. Information gleaned from the screening, brief intervention, and referral to treatment approach is limited and less beneficial than a thorough biopsychosocial assessment.

120. B: Maintaining confidentially is a potential challenge in using e-delivery for Debra's counseling services. It is noted that Debra's children frequently interrupt her sessions. Because Debra receives individual therapy rather than family therapy, maintaining confidentiality is a potential limitation. There is no indication that Debra is unable to make her own treatment decisions—that autonomy is not honored. The therapeutic alliance also appears unaffected by e-therapy. Although Cheryl may not provide evidence-based practices, this is unrelated to electronic service delivery.

121. D: Anxiety disorder warrants consideration as a differential diagnosis. Debra's symptoms include worry, irritability, difficulty concentrating, and sleep disturbances, all of which are criteria for anxiety disorder. Although insomnia and difficulty concentrating are associated with major depressive disorder, there is no evidence of depressed mood. Similarly, PTSD criteria include concentration difficulties; however, no traumatic event is noted. Oppositional defiant disorder often co-occurs with ADHD in children. Although Debra can be short tempered and irritable, oppositional defiant disorder can be ruled out because there is no evidence of argumentative or vindictive behavior. To diagnose a mental disorder, Cheryl would need to determine that the disorder is not attributed to substance use or another medical condition and establish the duration of symptoms (e.g., 6 months for anxiety disorder).

122. C: Chronic and prolonged use of marijuana is associated with cognitive impairment (a lowered IQ). Research suggests that frequent marijuana use among adolescents can lower IQ scores between 2 and 8 points. Heart damage is a symptom of chronic methamphetamine use. Malnourishment is common with prolonged cocaine use, whereas slurred speech results from opioid or alcohol intoxication.

123. C: Clients with a history of abuse often have painful and difficult memories and feelings about relationships. Abuse often occurs in close relationships where the client should have been safe and protected. As the therapeutic bond in counseling grows, emerging feelings of closeness and trust can often trigger the complex feelings of the past. In so doing, these painful past feelings may be projected onto the counselor, causing the relationship to deteriorate. Clients may cope by trying to avoid dealing with the past, or they may maneuver the counselor into interactive patterns that replicate the past (e.g., caretaker, abuser, neglector). Care should be used not be manipulated, however unintentionally, into a client's past relational roles. This is best accomplished by maintaining objectivity, avoiding being drawn into offered roles, and by dealing directly and openly with any transference issues that arise.

124. C: Clients in the preparation stage of change (SOC) would benefit from a menu of options. In the precontemplation SOC, the client does not indicate that there is a problem and has no intention to change. Counselors guide clients in the precontemplation stage by helping them increase self-awareness. During the contemplation stage, clients consider the possibility of a problem, but fall short of acknowledging its full extent. Interventions in this stage include normalizing ambivalence and "tipping the decisional balance scales." Clients in the preparation SOC recognize that there is a problem and express a desire to change. Counselors intervene in this stage by providing clients with a menu of options. The action SOC is characterized by the client making specific changes to their behavior. Counselors work with clients in this stage by reinforcing positive change and helping clients remain motivated.

125. A: According to the integrated developmental model of supervision, a counselor's professional development is measured in the areas of awareness, motivation, and autonomy, which provide overarching structures useful for determining the counselor's developmental level. At Level 1, the counselor is self-focused (i.e., awareness), high in anxiety (i.e., motivation), and dependent on the supervisor (i.e., autonomous). At Level 2, the counselor is less self-focused and more client-focused (i.e., awareness), vacillates between hesitancy and confidence (i.e., motivation), and becomes less dependent on the supervisor (i.e., autonomous). Level 3 counselors remain focused on the client and self-aware of interpersonal dynamics (i.e., awareness), display increased confidence (i.e., motivation), and exhibit increased independence while remaining open to supervisory feedback (i.e., autonomous). There is also a Level 3i in which the counselor has integrated skills across all domains.

126. C: Virtually all psychoactive substances that cross the blood-brain barrier will affect the fetus, with some associated with dependency and withdrawals at birth. However, alcohol is more harmful to the developing fetus than marijuana, amphetamines, and methadone. Even moderate drinking during pregnancy (particularly during the first trimester) can result in congenital disabilities such as organ and skeletal malformations and intellectual impairment. The potential for life-long harm, including learning and behavior problems, can occur with heavier use. More regular alcohol abuse may result in fetal alcohol syndrome (FAS), often with characteristic head and facial deformities, intellectual impairments, heart defects, and memory, vision, and hearing problems. Fetal alcohol spectrum disorders refer to the mix of problems associated with prenatal alcohol exposure. Prenatal exposure to marijuana can lead to complications later in life, such as memory impairments, difficulty attending to tasks, and behavioral issues. Pregnant mothers with methamphetamine use may experience poor appetite, placing the infant at risk for premature birth and low birth weight. Lastly, methadone is an approved drug for pregnant women with opioid use disorder, with little evidence citing poor fetal outcomes when used as prescribed.

127. D: The primary purpose of substance abuse assessment is to develop a full understanding of the severity and extent of substance use. The he assessment process should also identify and explore other closely related issues such as co-occurring disorders (both mental and physical), the onset of substance use, current stressors, employment and education, interpersonal and familial relationships, and other social and legal concerns. The overarching goal of assessment is to gather sufficient information to establish (1) a working diagnosis of current substance abuse, (2) significant co-occurring disorders, (3) the quality and availability of important supports, (4) readiness for change, and (5) all other necessary information sufficient to establish a meaningful and successful treatment plan.

128. A: Principle 1-23 of The NAADAC Code of Ethics (2021) states that APs must refrain from sexual relationships with current or former clients, saying, "Addiction professionals shall not engage in any form of sexual or romantic relationship with any current or former client, nor shall they accept as a client anyone with whom they have engaged in a romantic, sexual, social, or familial relationship." This principle applies to face-to-face and electronic interactions.

129. C: Community reinforcement training (CRT) improves the likelihood of entering and remaining in treatment. The community-reinforcement approach (CRA) supports abstinence by eliminating reinforcements for drinking and enhancing reinforcements for sobriety. An extension of this, the community reinforcement and family training (CRAFT) program teaches positive behavior rewards to encourage and support treatment. Families learn how to make sober activities more attractive and drug- or alcohol-using activities less inviting. They also learn to stop rescuing their loved one and instead allow the user to fully experience natural consequences. Clients entering treatment through confrontation are more likely to relapse than those encouraged into treatment. Family members also benefit by developing greater independence and learning skills that reduce symptoms of anger, anxiety, and depression, even if their loved one does not accept treatment. CRAFT is culturally sensitive and works within a client's values and beliefs to develop a successful treatment plan. CRAFT research reveals that nearly seven of ten people using the program will successfully motivate a substance-using loved one to attend treatment.

130. C: A case manager must engage in cultural self-assessment to gain cultural competence for interacting with clients. Experts have identified five elements related to attaining cultural competence. One is to understand the dynamics involved in cultural interactions; another is the cultural self-assessment. A third element is not only to be aware of diversity, but moreover to respect and value it. However, this respect and valuation does not take the place of or eliminate the fourth element, which is the need for the case manager to add cultural knowledge into their repertoire of skills. The fifth element is the case manager's ability and success in adapting practices to settings marked by diversity, rather than using the same practices regardless of setting.

131. D: A number of evidence-based prevention programs have been designed to target youth in various settings. There are three types of youth substance abuse prevention programs: (1) universal programs—designed to address both risk and protective factors in the general community or in school settings; (2) selective programs—oriented to engage youth that possess specifically identified risk factors that increase their likelihood of developing a substance use disorder; and (3) indicated programs—designed to address issues relevant to youth who currently engage in substance use. Central to all these programs is education regarding the harms caused by substances as such education has proven to reduce experimentation and lower the rates of continued substance use among youth.

132. D: Intense and periodic cravings are a criterion for impaired control over use. The DSM-5-TR uses the following criteria to assess the presence and severity of SUD: (1) impaired control over use (including consuming large amounts of the substance or consuming the substance for a longer period than intended), the desire to control use, time spent on substance-related activities and recovery, and an intense desire or craving to use; (2) social impairment (which consists of functional impairment at work, home, or school), using the substance despite negative social consequences, and giving up on activities (e.g., social, work, or recreational) because of substance use; (3) risky use, which involves using the substance in dangerous or physically hazardous situations and continuing to use the substance knowing of its adverse effects; and (4) pharmacologic symptoms including tolerance and withdrawal.

133. D: The Screening, Brief Intervention, and Referral to Treatment (SBIRT) public health approach is designed for use in hospital emergency departments, trauma centers, primary care clinics, and other health care settings. The goal is to identify diagnosable substance abuse disorders as well as those at-risk for developing a disorder before serious consequences develop. Each key component has a specific function toward this end: (1) screening—identifying and rapidly assessing substance use severity and determining the appropriate treatment level needed; (2) brief intervention—enhancing clients' awareness and insights regarding substance abuse consequences as well as motivating the client toward behavioral change; (3) referral to treatment—linking clients to specialized substance abuse treatment options as assessment indicates is needed and appropriate.

134. C: Barbiturates carry an increased risk of psychological dependence when taken for sleep. Barbiturates are central nervous system (CNS) depressants and can be addictive even when used as prescribed. Barbiturates are highly toxic and known to have a narrow therapeutic index, which reflects the range between a drug's toxicity and therapeutic dose. Additionally, barbiturates can cause psychological dependence when higher doses are taken daily for one month. Barbiturates pass into the brain through the bloodstream and can depress physiological functions such as breathing. If too much of a barbiturate is taken, the depressive effect can be enough to stop breathing and other functions entirely.

135. D: In addition to alcohol and nicotine, Anthony reports using spice, which has a street name of K2, inhalants, known as whippets, and marijuana, or weed. Street names for ketamine include special k, kit kat, purple, jet, ket, and vitamin K.

136. C: A correlational relationship exists between ADHD and SUD. Individuals diagnosed with ADHD are twice as likely to develop SUD than their peers without ADHD. The link between ADHD stimulant medication and developing SUD and addiction occurring with higher doses is unfounded.

137. C: The prefrontal cortex is underdeveloped in adolescents. This area of the brain is responsible for decision-making, planning, and impulse control and is not fully mature until age 25, creating more opportunities for risky behaviors (e.g., drug use). Other parts of the brain that develop first include the cerebellum, which is responsible for coordination, motor skills, and physical activity; the nucleus accumbens, which controls motivation; and the amygdala, which is responsible for emotion, memories, and the stress response.

138. A: Dopamine is the neurotransmitter that is primarily responsible for motivating individuals to engage in substance use. Surges in dopamine cause feelings of pleasure and intense euphoria. Triggers and environmental cues are caused by paired associations with substance use, which were likely responsible for Anthony's desire to use while out in his neighborhood. Gamma-aminobutyric acid is responsible for slowed neuronal activity, anxiety, and anesthesia. Norepinephrine is responsible for arousal, mood, and the stress response.

139. D: A common intensive outpatient treatment (IOT) program involves three hours of treatment on three days or evenings each week. Other programs meet five days or evenings per week. The schedule might involve back-to-back ninety-minute groups on two evenings. One provides opportunities for those in a similar recovery stage to share daily concerns, and the other might involve a psychoeducational topic. A third evening might include an hour-long skills training group, thirty minutes of individual counseling, and a ninety-minute family session. Group sessions are often ninety minutes, though the duration may vary according to need and group responsiveness. Psychoeducational sessions often consist of thirty-minute lectures followed by fifteen-minute question-and-answer periods. The shorter duration ensures client attention to instruction. Interactive group treatment periods are more engaging and thus more easily sustained for longer sessions. The expected duration of active treatment in IOT programs varies, but many span twelve to sixteen weeks. After active treatment concludes, clients step down to a maintenance phase that may extend for six months or more.

140. A: Intoxication with alcohol, tranquilizers, and opioids all include the symptom of low blood pressure. Ataxia (i.e., difficult or "drunk"-appearing gait, and disinhibition) is more symptomatic of intoxication with alcohol and tranquilizers than with opioids. Nystagmus (i.e., unusual eye movements) is a frequent symptom of intoxication from tranquilizers rather than alcohol or opioids. None of these symptoms are associated with amphetamine intoxication.

141. B: Case management offers continuity by providing clients with a single, organized contact point. This allows for the availability of multiple services for one client. Instead of involving a complicated and disorganized process of referrals to unconnected, independent agencies, case management offers the client services from multiple agencies a single, organized service. Rather than spreading responsibility for the client across all agencies, case management consolidates the responsibility to the case manager, giving the client a single point of contact and hence greater continuity of service. The case manager is obligated not only to the client but also to all members of the agencies and systems they interact with on the client's behalf.

142. A: Nootropics, also known as "smart drugs", are designed to boost memory and cognitive performance. These neuro-enhancing drugs are known to enhance concentration, focus, and memory and to help ward off fatigue and somnolence. Nootropics can be natural, synthetic, obtained with a prescription. Dietary or natural supplements include ginseng and gingko. Among the more popular prescription medications are Provigil (generic: modafinil) and Adderall (generic: dextroamphetamine saccharate, amphetamine aspartate, dextroamphetamine sulfate, and amphetamine sulfate—or, sometimes, just amphetamine/dextroamphetamine). Adderall contains amphetamine salts designed to increase dopamine and norepinephrine levels in the brain and is used in the treatment of attention deficit hyperactivity disorder (ADHD). Provigil is a stimulant used in the treatment of sleep disorders. Another nootropic, Piracetam (or nootropil; generic: 2-oxo-1-pyrrolidine acetamide), is sold as a supplement. Chemically, it influences neuronal and vascular functions and thereby enhances cognitive function without acting as a sedative or stimulant. It has been used to treat depression, the disabling effects of stroke, and a variety of other neurological disorders.

143. D: Homeostasis refers to the process of creating family balance through equilibrium. Don Jackson coined the term and likened families to an artistic mobile in which movement in one part causes movement in others, with the whole tending to return to an original configuration. When applied to a person with substance disorder, homeostasis is maintained when change is restricted and substance use is maintained, and disrupted (into a state of disequilibrium) when clients change patterns of substance use. In general, family systems that include a person with a substance use disorder are ridged. Children quickly blame themselves for pain and problems and rigidly play out their roles in the family paradigm. Virginia Satir identified family roles when under stress and labeled them: the "blamer," the "placater," the "irrelevant," and the "super-reasonable." Wegscheider (1981) added the "family hero" (usually the oldest), the "scapegoat," (acts out to divert attention from the family problem), the "lost child" who is withdrawn, and the "mascot" (often the youngest) who distracts with humor and fun, but is often insecure, fearful, and lonely.

144. C: Harm reduction strategies have proven to be effective for viral hepatitis, OUD, and HIV. Harm reduction is used to lessen the consequences of substance use, including overdose deaths, sexually transmitted infections, infections spread through IV drug use, incarceration, and unemployment. Harm reduction strategies may include increased education and testing, needle exchange programs, antiretroviral therapy for HIV, overdose reversal (e.g., naloxone), psychoeducation, and condom distribution.

145. B: The highest confidentiality protection for clients with co-occurring disorders is 42 CFR Part 2. The regulations offered by 42 CFR Part 2 protect client records from unauthorized disclosures for clients with substance use disorder, which include individuals diagnosed with both mental disorders and substance use disorders (i.e., co-occurring disorders). This is designed to protect clients seeking treatment from negative consequences, including job loss, criminal prosecution, or loss of child custody. HIPAA offers the same confidentiality protections for the records of all individuals, with key elements including protections for electronic health records. The Individuals with Disabilities Act, or PL 94-142, provides all students with free and reduced public education delivered in the least restrictive environment. Section 504 of the Rehabilitation Act of 1973 offers federal protection for individuals with disabilities from discrimination. It ensures that accommodations are provided for individuals with impairments that substantially limit life activities.

146. B: Physiological dependence exists if tolerance or withdrawal is in evidence. Tolerance is in evidence if there is a need for significantly more of the involved substance to achieve a desired effect or intoxication or if the effects of the substance are significantly diminished when the same amount of the substance is used. Withdrawal is in evidence if abstinence induces a withdrawal syndrome as expected for the substance or the same substance (or one closely related chemically) is used to relieve or ward off withdrawal symptoms.

147. A: The Matrix Model (also referred to as neurobehavioral treatment) was formulated during the 1980s' to treat cocaine and methamphetamine use. The model utilizes a complementary set of evidence-based practices coordinated and delivered as a program. Drawing upon cognitive-behavioral therapy, motivational interviewing, and findings from relapse prevention literature, combined with educational support and twelve-step program involvement, the model seeks to coordinate and optimize evidence-based treatments and support resources. Guiding principles include: (1) developing a positive therapeutic relationship; (2) applying a scheduled structure and expectations; (3) educating participants and families regarding brain chemistry, cravings, recovery, and relapse prevention; (4) incorporating cognitive-behavioral concepts for change; (5) reinforcing positive behavioral changes; (6) outlining the expected course of treatment and recovery; (7) promoting self-help (twelve-step) participation; and (8) using regular urine screenings.

148. C: To date, the FDA has approved medication assisted therapy for opioid use disorder and alcohol use disorder. The medications reduce cravings, inhibit the intoxicating effects, produce aversion, and lessen the desire to use the target substance. Medications for opioid use disorder include buprenorphine, methadone, and naltrexone. For individuals with alcohol use disorder, medication assisted therapy may include the following FDA approved medications: acamprosate, disulfiram, and naltrexone. There are currently no effective medications for the treatment of dependence on stimulants such as cocaine, marijuana, inhalants, or hallucinogens. There are medications to modestly mitigate the difficult withdrawal symptoms caused by these substances. For example, symptoms of stimulant withdrawal include insomnia, agitation, anxiety, and even delirium, psychosis, and hyperthermia in particularly acute cases. Neuroleptic medications can lessen the symptoms of psychosis and delirium, and benzodiazepines can reduce the symptoms of agitation and anxiety. Beyond symptom management, however, there are no target treatment drugs for these substances.

149. A: Working with substance abuse clients can expose counselors to high emotions, great volatility, emotionally traumatic narratives of abuse, and so on. Over time, counselors can develop symptoms of compassion fatigue, apathy, and discouragement. Left unchecked, such feelings can compromise the counselor's skills, erode relationships, and can lead to a greatly shortened professional career and diminished personal life success. To combat burnout, counselors should: (1) avoid working in isolation; (2) maintain close supervisory support; (3) look for debriefing opportunities; (4) carry a varied caseload to minimize overload in one emotional area; (5) avoid overload in the number of cases being seen; (6) keep personal and professional life separated; (7) take appropriate vacations and time off; and (8) consider attending a counselor support group. Psychotherapy can also help the counselor professionally and personally in such situations.

150. C: The Code of Federal Regulations (CFR) Title 42 Part 2 deals with issues of confidentiality when working with clients being treated for substance abuse. The confidentiality restrictions apply: (1) to records, which may not be disclosed even in administrative, civil, criminal, or legislative proceedings by any governmental authority; (2) to communications, even if the person seeking information already has it, could otherwise obtain it, is an official or law officer, has a subpoena, or otherwise claims the right of information release not permitted in the CFR; and (3) to acknowledgements concerning the presence of a client in a treatment facility, unless the client is in a setting that is not solely dedicated to substance abuse, at which point no admission of drug or alcohol treatment can be made. This also applies to any past, current, or anticipated substance abuse treatment.

It's Your Moment, Let's Celebrate It!

Share your story @mometrixtestpreparation